BRIAN CARTHY
THE CHAMPIONSHIP 2004
FOOTBALL AND HURLING • THE COMPLETE RECORD

Tomás Ó Sé, Kerry

DEDICATED TO

TRISH, JOHN BRIAN & SARAH MARIE

AND TO THE MEMORY OF TYRONE CAPTAIN, CORMAC MCANALLEN

& FORMER GALWAY ALL-IRELAND WINNING CAPTAIN, ENDA COLLERAN,

WHO BOTH SADLY DIED THIS YEAR.

By the same author, Brian Carthy:

Football Captains 1940-1993
The Championship 1995 – Football and Hurling
The Championship 1996 – Football and Hurling
The Championship 1997 – Football and Hurling
The Championship 1998 – Football and Hurling
The Championship 1999 – Football and Hurling
The Championship 2000 – Football and Hurling
The Championship 2001 – Football and Hurling
The Championship 2002 – Football and Hurling
The Championship 2003 – Football and Hurling

All Championship books listed above from 1997 onwards
plus *Championship 2004* are available from:

Sliabh Bán Productions,
P.O. Box No. 6369,
Fortfield, Dublin 6W.

BRIAN CARTHY
THE **CHAMPIONSHIP** 2004
FOOTBALL AND HURLING • THE COMPLETE RECORD

SLIABH BÁN PRODUCTIONS,
P.O. BOX NO. 6369,
FORTFIELD, DUBLIN 6W.

ISBN 0-9545829-1-8

A CIP record of this book is available from the British Library.

Cover Design: Martin McNamara, Temple of Design
Photography: Sportsfile, Russell Pritchard
Layout and Design: Mary Guinan, Temple of Design
Printed in Ireland by Future Print
Front Cover Photos: Matty Forde, (Wexford), Ciarán McDonald (Mayo),
Henry Shefflin (Kilkenny), Colm Cooper (Kerry), Seán Óg Ó hAilpín (Cork)

ACKNOWLEDGEMENTS

The author and publisher would like to thank all the people who assisted with the publication of this book.
Special thanks to Paddy Goode, Louise Brennan, Evan Hickey, Mary Guinan; to all our advertisers
and to Ray McManus and his Sportsfile team for permission to use their photographs.

CONTENTS

THE 2004 FOOTBALL CHAMPIONSHIP

THE 2004 HURLING CHAMPIONSHIP

Bank of Ireland
Football Championship

INTRODUCTION

Time moves on but it appears some things never change as evidenced by this year's championships which saw football kingpins Kerry win their 33rd All-Ireland title and Cork hurlers move one ahead of rivals Kilkenny in the roll of honour with 29 titles. Both counties can look back with pride on their performances in Championship 2004, as there is no doubt whatsoever but that the respective teams were under the spotlight like never before, approaching final days in Croke Park in September.

Kerry were clearly on a mission to exorcise the ghosts of those failures against Meath in the semi-final of 2001, Armagh in the 2002 decider and Tyrone in last year's semi-final while Cork were determined to make amends for that shattering All-Ireland final loss to Kilkenny twelve months previously.

Surprisingly, both showpieces were lop-sided encounters, with the winners in both instances having plenty to spare at the finish. Kerry completely overwhelmed Connacht champions Mayo to win by eight points while Cork restricted Kilkenny to just two points in the second half, a '65 and a free, both from Henry Shefflin, on their way to an eight points victory over the reigning champions. Kilkenny failed to score from play in the second half and were held scoreless for the final twenty-five minutes as Cork produced an awesome display of power, pace and skill.

It was a far cry from that late June Sunday at Semple Stadium, when Cork lost by a single point to a magnificent Waterford side in a classic Munster final. The fact that Cork went down by such a narrow margin against a truly superb team, held little sway with some supporters and media who were critical of the players and management. That criticism only served to make Donal O'Grady and his players more focused and determined as they set about reviving their Championship season. Cork travelled to Fitzgerald Stadium in Killarney on Saturday, July 10th, and showed true grit and determination to beat Tipperary by six points in Round 3 of the All-Ireland qualifiers. It was a testing game and the manner of their victory restored Cork's confidence.

Dinny Cahill gave the Leesiders extra incentive ahead of the counties' All-Ireland quarter-final meeting when he questioned the ability of some of the Rebel players, but the tactic backfired on the Antrim manager and his side suffered a twenty-two points trouncing.

Cork were equally as devastating in the semi-final and dished out an eighteen points drubbing to Leinster Champions Wexford, who learned the harsh realities of life in hurling's fast lane.

Cork denied Kilkenny the three-in-a-row with a powerhouse second half display to win emphatically by 0-17 to 0-9 and earn the title as the best hurling team in the land. The colour was certainly red and white in Croke Park at the finish and the roar that greeted Brian Corcoran's tight-angled shot that soared over the crossbar was testimony to the esteem in which the Erins Own man is held and the passion that Cork hurling engenders.

There were thirty-three games in the 2004 Guinness Hurling Championship, which was significant for the fact that it produced the first ever 'all back door final'.

Wexford defeated Kilkenny in the Leinster semi-final through a late goal from Mick Jacob and then moved on to beat Offaly in the provincial decider in early July by four points. Wexford subsequently lost heavily to Cork while Kilkenny turned their season around with a massive nineteen points victory over Galway in Round 3 of the qualifiers. Kilkenny were pushed to the very limit of their endurance before claiming a replay win over Clare in the All-Ireland quarter-final and Brian Cody's men then ended Waterford dreams with a narrow three points semi-final win. Antrim won the Ulster title with a 3-14 to 0-18 win over Down after a replay and joined Wexford and Waterford, who produced the performance of the summer to beat Cork in the Munster decider, as the 2004 provincial champions.

A new Championship format, as proposed by the high-powered Hurling Development committee will be in place for the 2005 season and it should prove hugely beneficial for the development of the game.

Cork showed in 2004 that adversity could be overcome with style, skill and confidence. Donal O'Grady's role in restoring pride in the Cork jersey was immense and should never be forgotten. He took charge at a difficult time for Cork hurling following the players' strike and brought them to an All-Ireland final in 2003 that resulted in a loss to Kilkenny. There was further heartbreak in late June of this year when the team went down by just a single point to Waterford in a riveting Munster Final. However, O'Grady remained calm, assured and confident and showed total belief in the team, and the players to a man repaid his faith by delivering the Liam McCarthy Cup in impressive fashion.

There was surprise but not shock some three weeks after that momentous September Sunday when O'Grady stepped down as Cork manager. The St. Finbarr's man had indicated earlier that when his commitments to Cork hurling in 2004 were complete, he would step aside and that he duly did with the same quiet dignity that he displayed throughout his term as Cork senior hurling manager.

Anyone who watched Kerry footballers endure such traumatic experiences in Croke Park in the 2001, 2002 and 2003 championships could not but be suitably impressed by their new found confidence and exuberance throughout the 2004 League and Championship campaigns. New manager Jack O'Connor has to be fully commended for the manner in which he had his team prepared to face all challenges and it resulted in a clean sweep of National League, Munster and All-Ireland titles.

Kerry began their championship campaign with an unconvincing display against Clare at Cusack Park in Ennis but still won by 2-10 to 0-9 and then brushed aside the tame Cork challenge in the semi-final by 0-15 to 0-7 in Killarney.

Kerry were extremely fortunate to draw with Limerick in the Munster Final at the Gaelic Grounds and then had to display even greater resilience to see off the challenge of Liam Kearns' side in the replay. It was on then to Croke Park for Jack O'Connor's side who recorded a 1-15 to 1-8 All-Ireland quarter-final win over Dublin, which was followed by an impressive 1-17 to 1-11 victory over surprise packets Derry in the semi-final.

It was like old times in Croke Park on Sunday, September 26, as Kerry produced an awesome display to power past a disappointing Mayo side in the final to claim their 33rd All-Ireland title.

There were 65 games in the 2004 Bank of Ireland Football Championship, which produced provincial final wins for Kerry, Mayo, Westmeath and Armagh, who defeated Donegal in the Ulster final, which was played in Croke Park. Clearly, Westmeath's first ever Leinster title success, following a 0-12 to 0-10 final victory after a replay over defending champions Laois, garnered most headlines. The success-starved supporters from the Lake County hailed manager Páidí Ó Sé a hero.

Fermanagh footballers were a revelation in Championship 2004 and recorded notable victories over Meath, Cork, Donegal and All-Ireland favourites, Armagh, before their amazing run came to an end against Mayo in a replay at the All-Ireland semi-final stage.

But the sad death of Tyrone captain Cormac McAnallen, who died suddenly at his home at the age of twenty-four last March, overshadowed the entire sporting year. His untimely death stunned the sporting community and his passing has left a huge void in the lives of his family, friends, team-mates and everyone who knew him. Last October, the G.A.A. and the A.F.L. decided that the Cup for the winners of the International Rules series would be dedicated to the memory of the late lamented All-Star footballer, who had represented his country with such pride and distinction.

This is the tenth edition of my book, which once again features every single game in both the Hurling and Football Championships with all the relevant statistical details. Thanks for your continued support through the years.

BRIAN CARTHY

NÓ BÓTHER
CROKE PARK

ON THE ROAD AGAIN.

It's a new season. A time when all roads can lead to glory.
But in the end, where only the strongest will ever tread.
It's a time of new expectations against old rivals. A time
when new belief confronts old demons. It's a time full of
new possibilities. It's that time again.

The AIB GAA Club Championships.

be with **AIB**

Dara Ó Cinnéide, Kerry

2004 ALL-IRELAND SENIOR FOOTBALL FINAL REPORT

Kerry claimed their 33rd All-Ireland title with a comprehensive eight points victory over a Mayo side that were simply unable to raise their standard to meet the awesome challenge of the Munster Champions. Kerry took control at midfield and other crucial areas from the very start and never once relinquished their grip with a display of pace and skill that overwhelmed John Maughan's team. Kerry were sharper to the breaking ball and despite the fillip of a 5th minute goal from Alan Dillon, it became increasingly evident that Mayo were powerless to cope with the pressure being applied from all sectors by the rampant Kerrymen. Ultimately, it turned out to be a no-contest final and such was Kerry's dominance from the second quarter onwards, it was apparent that Mayo were going to struggle to mount a serious challenge. Ciarán McDonald kicked over a wonderful long range point from the right wing, which preceded Dillon's goal, but that was about as good as it got for the Connacht Champions. McDonald, who scored three points, showed flashes of his undoubted genius throughout but, as the game wore on and as Kerry became more dominant, the brilliant Crossmolina man had to move further and further outfield to gain even limited possession.

Special mention, first and foremost, for William Kirby, who was magnificent at midfield for Kerry and contributed no less than three points from play. Kirby's display was even more notable for the fact that the Austin Stacks man would have been hard pressed to make the starting line-up had Darragh Ó Sé, ruled out with an ankle injury, being available for selection.

It was an All-Ireland final to savour for Kirby, who was at midfield when Kerry, inspired by Maurice Fitzgerald, defeated Mayo in the 1997 All-Ireland Final.

One of the real gentlemen of sport, Johnny Crowley, who came on for the injured Billy O'Shea in that 1997 decider, more than justified his selection ahead of Mike Frank Russell, with a powerful creative display that helped pave the way for Kerry's victory. Crowley used his strength and experience as the target man to win vital possession and linked up seamlessly with the outstanding and naturally gifted Colm 'Gooch' Cooper, who himself scored 1-5 and team captain, Dara Ó Cinnéide, who contributed eight points in a hugely impressive outing. Tomás Ó Sé, the finest wing back in the game at the present time, further enhanced his reputation with a highly impressive performance.

Kerry goalkeeper Diarmuid Murphy could not be faulted for the two Mayo goals and embellished a rock solid display with stunning saves from Michael Conroy and Trevor Mortimer. Tom O'Sullivan, Michael McCarthy along with one of the real stars of

Championship 2004, Aidan O'Mahony, all ruled their patch for long stages while in front of them Tomás Ó Sé, Marc Ó Sé, who landed a point from play, and Eamon Fitzmaurice more than played their part in Kerry's victory. Fitzmaurice had the difficult task of trying to curb Ciarán McDonald but the Finuge player fared well against Mayo's most dangerous forward.

William Kirby reigned supreme at midfield and Eoin Brosnan was also highly effective as Kerry controlled that vital sector against Fergal Kelly and Ronan McGarrity, who both worked hard but to no avail. David Brady added strength to the sector when introduced in place of Kelly in the 23rd minute, but there was no stopping Kirby and Brosnan, such was their dominance.

Paul Galvin, another real find for Kerry this season, impressed greatly with his strong running and scored a point for good measure. Declan O'Sullivan, too, kicked over a point from play but his work-rate and general play were noteworthy factors in Kerry's overall team effort. As usual, Liam Hassett, the 1997 All-Ireland winning captain, worked tirelessly and had a right battle with one of Mayo's best defenders, Peadar Gardiner. As expected, Seamus Moynihan and Mike Frank Russell, both came off the bench to wild applause and their appearances further demoralised the Mayo players.

Kerry's new manager, Jack O'Connor along with his selectors, Johnny Culloty and Ger O'Keeffe and trainer Pat Flanagan deserve tremendous credit for having their players so well prepared, both physically and mentally, for an All-Ireland final that had so much at stake for the kingpins of football.

O'Connor, from the Dromid Pearses club, has proved to be an inspirational manager and the fact that he guided Kerry to a National League title and All-Ireland Championship success in his first year in charge is testimony to his ability as a coach.

It was a quite remarkable turnaround in Kerry's football fortunes considering the Croke Park failures of the previous three seasons. Kerry went down to Tyrone in last year's All-Ireland semi-final by seven points, 0-13 to 0-6; lost to Armagh in the All-Ireland final of 2002 by one point and were trounced by Meath in the 2001 semi-final by 2-14 to 0-5. Moreover, Kerry lined out against Mayo without three highly influential players: Darragh Ó Sé missed the match because of injury; Seamus Moynihan returned from a long-term injury to take his place on the bench while Mike Frank Russell lost out to Johnny Crowley.

It would have appeared an impossibility earlier in the year that Kerry would contest an All-Ireland final with a starting line-up minus Darragh Ó Sé, Moynihan and Russell and still win by eight points, But such was the resilience and character within the side, hardened and primed for Championship fare by O'Connor, that by the time Moynihan and Russell were introduced from the bench, the game was effectively over. Mayo manager, John Maughan kindly joined me on 'The Championship' programme on R.T.E. Radio One after the match in Croke Park on the Sunday evening and made no excuses. Maughan, who has given so much of his life to Mayo football, conceded that Kerry were the superior team.

The crucial score of the final came in the 25th minute when Cooper scored a spectacular goal to lift Kerry eight points clear, 1-11 to 1-03. It could have been even worse for Mayo eight minutes later when the in-form Johnny Crowley was denied a goal by Peter Burke, who brought off a magnificent save. Cooper scored 1-2 from play in the first half while Marc Ó Sé, William Kirby and Declan O'Sullivan each sent over a point from play.

Dara Ó Cinnéide converted a '45 before half time to bring his tally to seven points – four from play – and leave Kerry comfortably ahead at the break by 1-12 to 1-4.

Mayo had scored 1-2 of their first half total by the 11th minute and could only accumulate two points from frees for the remainder of the half from Ciarán McDonald – a magnificent point with the outside of the boot -and one from Alan Dillon. Two pointed frees in 24 minutes underlined Mayo's shortage of scoring options.

Conor Mortimer shot over the bar with a goal chance on early in the second half and any remote chance of a Mayo revival was dashed when Kirby, Cooper and Ó Cinnéide scored a point apiece to continue Kerry's dominant phase of open attacking football.

Kerry had surged eleven points clear within thirteen minutes of the re-start, 1-16 to 1-5 and the game was long over as a contest when impressive substitute Michael Conroy scored a late goal for the demoralised Connacht champions, many of whose supporters had left the ground by the time Pat McEnaney blew the full-time whistle.

It was a special victory for Kerry and all the heartbreak of the previous three seasons was forgotten when their captain, Dara Ó Cinnéide from An Ghaeltacht, raised the Sam Maguire Cup like his club man and former county manager, Páidí Ó Sé some nineteen years earlier.

The old order was restored once again and Kerry were back at the top table following victories over Clare, Cork, Limerick, after a replay, Dublin, Derry and Mayo.

It was a season to savour for this proud football county, which now boasts a record thirty-three All-Ireland titles, eleven more than nearest rivals Dublin in the most famous roll of honour in Irish sport.

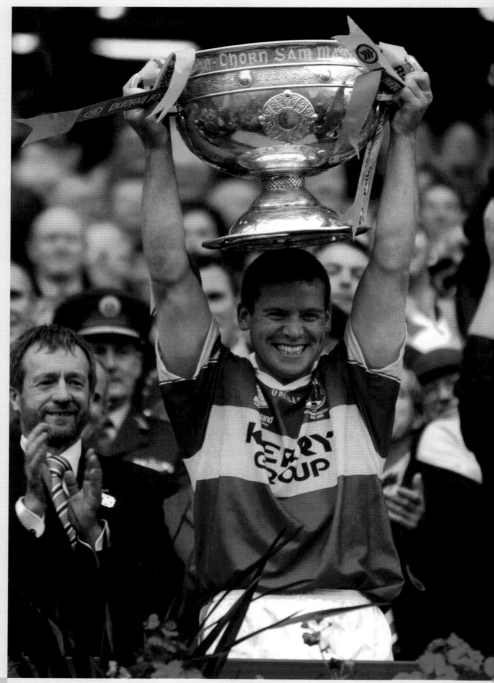

Kerry Captain Dara Ó Cinnéide

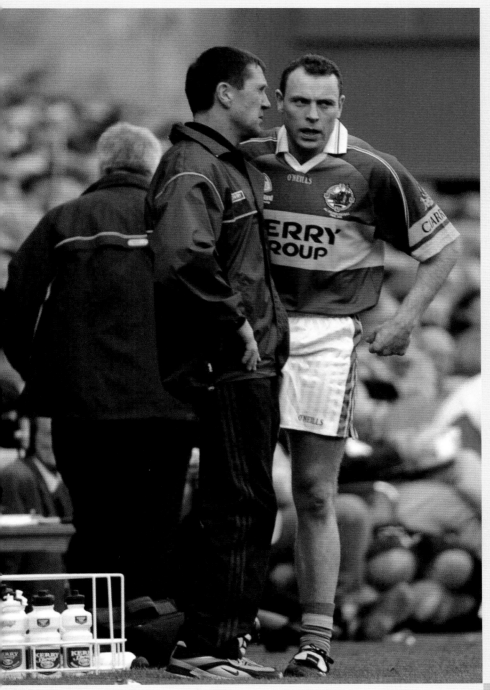

Kerry Manager, Jack O'Connor and Seamus Moynihan

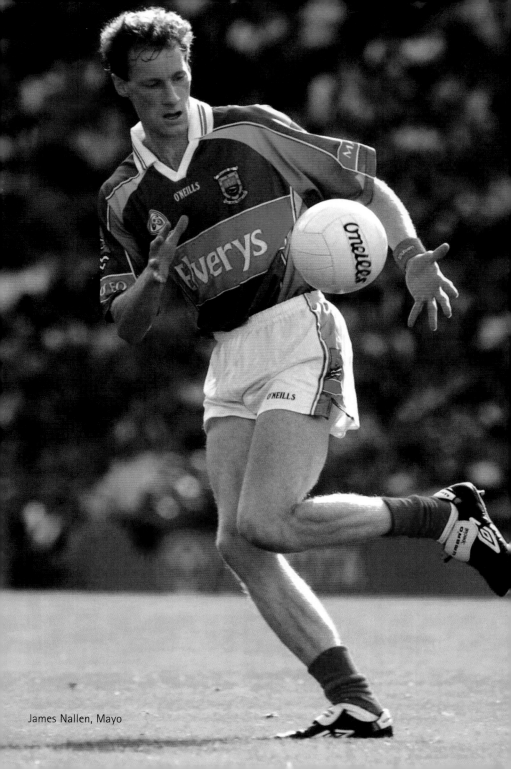

James Nallen, Mayo

ALL-IRELAND SENIOR FOOTBALL CHAMPIONSHIP FINAL

KERRY VERSUS MAYO
CROKE PARK
REFEREE: PAT MCENANEY (MONAGHAN)
RESULT: KERRY 1-20   MAYO 2-9

SCORERS – KERRY: Dara Ó Cinnéide 0-8; Colm Cooper 1-5; William Kirby 0-3; Declan O'Sullivan 0-1; Mike Frank Russell 0-1; Paul Galvin 0-1; Marc Ó Sé 0-1

SCORERS – MAYO: Alan Dillon 1-2; Michael Conroy 1-1; Ciarán McDonald 0-3; Brian Maloney 0-1; Andy Moran 0-1; Conor Mortimer 0-1

KERRY

Diarmuid Murphy

Aidan O'Mahony   Michael McCarthy   Tom O'Sullivan

Marc Ó Sé   Eamon Fitzmaurice   Tomás Ó Sé

Eoin Brosnan   William Kirby

Liam Hassett   Declan O'Sullivan   Paul Galvin

Colm Cooper   Dara Ó Cinnéide (*Captain*)   Johnny Crowley

SUBSTITUTES: Seamus Moynihan for Liam Hassett;
Mike Frank Russell for Johnny Crowley; Ronan O'Connor for Dara Ó Cinnéide;
Paddy Kelly for Paul Galvin; Brendan Guiney for Tomás Ó Sé

MAYO

Peter Burke

Dermot Geraghty   David Heaney   Gary Ruane (*Captain*)

Peadar Gardiner   James Nallen   Pat Kelly

Ronan McGarrity   Fergal Kelly

Trevor Mortimer   Ciarán McDonald   Brian Maloney

Conor Mortimer   James Gill   Alan Dillon

SUBSTITUTES: David Brady for Fergal Kelly; Conor Moran for Dermot Geraghty;
Michael Conroy for James Gill; Andy Moran for Conor Mortimer;
Paddy Navin for David Heaney

Trevor Mortimer, May

Tom O'Sullivan, Kerry and Paddy Bradley, Derry

22nd August, Croke Park:
Mayo 0-9   Fermanagh 0-9 (A Draw)

28th August, Croke Park:
Mayo 0-13   Fermanagh 1-8 (Replay)

29th August, Croke Park:
Kerry 1-17   Derry 1-11

Barry Owens, Fermanagh

ALL-IRELAND SENIOR FOOTBALL CHAMPIONSHIP SEMI-FINAL

MAYO VERSUS FERMANAGH
CROKE PARK
REFEREE: MICHAEL COLLINS (CORK)
RESULT: MAYO 0-9 FERMANAGH 0-9 (A DRAW)

SCORERS – MAYO: Conor Mortimer 0-4; Alan Dillon 0-2; Trevor Mortimer 0-1; David Heaney 0-1; Ciarán McDonald 0-1

SCORERS – FERMANAGH: Colm Bradley 0-3; Eamonn Maguire 0-1; Stephen Maguire 0-1; James Sherry 0-1; Liam McBarron 0-1; Mark Little 0-1; Tom Brewster 0-1

MAYO
Peter Burke

Conor Moran   David Heaney   Gary Ruane (*Captain*)

Peadar Gardiner   James Nallen   Pat Kelly

Ronan McGarrity   David Brady

James Gill   Ciarán McDonald   Alan Dillon

Conor Mortimer   Trevor Mortimer   Brian Maloney

SUBSTITUTES: Andy Moran for Brian Maloney; Gary Mullins for David Brady; Marty McNicholas for Alan Dillon

FERMANAGH
Niall Tinney

Niall Bogue   Barry Owens   Ryan McCluskey

Raymond Johnston   Shane McDermott (*Captain*)   Peter Sherry

Marty McGrath   Liam McBarron

Eamonn Maguire   James Sherry   Mark Little

Ciarán O'Reilly   Stephen Maguire   Colm Bradley

SUBSTITUTES: Tom Brewster for Mark Little; Hughie Brady for Peter Sherry; Mark Murphy for James Sherry

ALL-IRELAND SENIOR FOOTBALL CHAMPIONSHIP
SEMI-FINAL REPLAY

MAYO VERSUS FERMANAGH
CROKE PARK
REFEREE: JOHN BANNON (LONGFORD)
RESULT: MAYO 0-13   FERMANAGH 1-8

SCORERS – MAYO: Conor Mortimer 0-5; Trevor Mortimer 0-3; Ciarán McDonald 0-2; Ronan McGarrity 0-1; David Brady 0-1; Austin O'Malley 0-1

SCORERS – FERMANAGH: James Sherry 1-1; Colm Bradley 0-3; Stephen Maguire 0-2; Mark Little 0-1; Tom Brewster 0-1

MAYO
Peter Burke

Conor Moran   David Heaney   Gary Ruane (*Captain*)

Peadar Gardiner   James Nallen   Pat Kelly

Ronan McGarrity   Fergal Kelly

James Gill   Ciarán McDonald   Alan Dillon

Conor Mortimer   Trevor Mortimer   Brian Maloney

SUBSTITUTES: Dermot Geraghty for Conor Moran; Austin O'Malley for Brian Maloney; David Brady for Fergal Kelly; Damien Munnelly for James Gill

FERMANAGH
Niall Tinney

Niall Bogue   Barry Owens   Ryan McCluskey

Raymond Johnston   Shane McDermott (*Captain*)   Peter Sherry

Marty McGrath   Liam McBarron

Eamonn Maguire   Stephen Maguire   Mark Little

Ciarán O'Reilly   Tom Brewster   Colm Bradley

SUBSTITUTES: Hughie Brady for Peter Sherry; James Sherry for Ciarán O'Reilly; Declan O'Reilly for Barry Owens

ALL-IRELAND SENIOR FOOTBALL CHAMPIONSHIP SEMI-FINAL

KERRY VERSUS DERRY
CROKE PARK
REFEREE: BRIAN WHITE (WEXFORD)
RESULT: KERRY 1-17 DERRY 1-11

SCORERS – KERRY: Colm Cooper 0-6; Declan O'Sullivan 1-0; Dara Ó Cinnéide 0-2; Mike Frank Russell 0-2; Tomás Ó Sé 0-2; William Kirby 0-1; Eoin Brosnan 0-1; Paul Galvin 0-1; Darragh Ó Sé 0-1; Paddy Kelly 0-1

SCORERS – DERRY: Paddy Bradley 0-6; Enda Muldoon 1-1; Conleith Gilligan 0-2; Paul McFlynn 0-1; Fergal Doherty 0-1

KERRY
Diarmuid Murphy

Marc Ó Sé   Michael McCarthy   Tom O'Sullivan

Aidan O'Mahony   Eamon Fitzmaurice   Tomás Ó Sé

Darragh Ó Sé   William Kirby

Liam Hassett   Eoin Brosnan   Paul Galvin

Colm Cooper   Dara Ó Cinnéide (*Captain*)   Declan O'Sullivan

SUBSTITUTES: Mike Frank Russell for Darragh Ó Sé; Paddy Kelly for Liam Hassett; Tommy Griffin for William Kirby; Johnny Crowley for Colm Cooper; Declan Quill for Dara Ó Cinnéide

DERRY
Barry Gillis

Kevin McGuckin   Niall McCusker   Seán Marty Lockhart (*Captain*)

Francis McEldowney   Paul McFlynn   Padraig Kelly

Fergal Doherty   Patsy Bradley

James Donaghy   Johnny McBride   Conleth Moran

Johnny Bradley   Paddy Bradley   Enda Muldoon

SUBSTITUTES: Gerard O'Kane for Francis McEldowney; Gavin Donaghy for Conleth Moran; Eamonn Burke for Johnny Bradley; Conleith Gilligan for James Donaghy; Mark Lynch for Johnny McBride

Heroes aren't born - they are made

Whether it's a brilliant save or a match winning poin
it all begins with the dedicated and committed people who nurture the heroes
tomorrow. As the sponsor of both Cumann na mBunscol and the Allianz Leagu
Allianz is proud to be associated with these and all the people who make the gam
the success they are.

Allianz ⑪
The Power On Your Side

7th August, Croke Park:
Mayo 0–16   Tyrone 1–9

7th August, Croke Park:
Fermanagh 0–12   Armagh 0–11

14th August, Croke Park:
Derry 2–9   Westmeath 0–13

14th August, Croke Park:
Kerry 1–15   Dublin 1–8

Mark Little, Fermanagh

Ciarán McDonald, Mayo

ALL-IRELAND SENIOR FOOTBALL CHAMPIONSHIP QUARTER-FINAL

MAYO VERSUS TYRONE
CROKE PARK
REFEREE: PADDY RUSSELL (TIPPERARY)
RESULT: MAYO 0–16   TYRONE 1–9

SCORERS – MAYO: Alan Dillon 0–6; David Brady 0–3; Conor Mortimer 0–3; Trevor Mortimer 0–2; Ciarán McDonald 0–1; Ronan McGarrity 0–1

SCORERS – TYRONE: Stephen O'Neill 1–3; Owen Mulligan 0–3; Mark Harte 0–1; Ger Cavlan 0–1; Peter Canavan 0–1

MAYO
Peter Burke

Conor Moran   David Heaney   Gary Ruane

Fergal Costello (*Captain*)   James Nallen   Peadar Gardiner

Ronan McGarrity   David Brady

James Gill   Ciarán McDonald   Alan Dillon

Conor Mortimer   Trevor Mortimer   Brian Maloney

SUBSTITUTES: Pat Kelly for Fergal Costello; Andy Moran for Conor Mortimer; Declan Sweeney for David Heaney; Austin O'Malley for Brian Maloney

TYRONE
Pascal McConnell

Ryan McMenamin   Conor Gormley   Michael McGee

Joe McMahon   Shane Sweeney   Philip Jordan

Kevin Hughes   Seán Cavanagh

Brian Dooher (*Captain*)   Ger Cavlan   Ciarán Gourley

Mark Harte   Owen Mulligan   Stephen O'Neill

SUBSTITUTES: Dermot Carlin for Conor Gormley; Peter Canavan for Shane Sweeney; Brian McGuigan for Mark Harte; Colm McCullagh for Michael McGee

ALL-IRELAND SENIOR FOOTBALL CHAMPIONSHIP QUARTER-FINAL

FERMANAGH VERSUS ARMAGH
CROKE PARK
REFEREE: JOHN BANNON (LONGFORD)
RESULT: FERMANAGH 0-12 ARMAGH 0-11

SCORERS – FERMANAGH: Stephen Maguire 0-5; Tom Brewster 0-3; Colm Bradley 0-2; James Sherry 0-1; Eamonn Maguire 0-1

SCORERS – ARMAGH: Steven McDonnell 0-7; Diarmaid Marsden 0-1; Paddy McKeever 0-1; Kieran McGeeney 0-1; Oisín McConville 0-1

FERMANAGH
Niall Tinney

Niall Bogue   Barry Owens   Ryan McCluskey

Raymond Johnston   Shane McDermott (*Captain*)   Peter Sherry

Marty McGrath   Liam McBarron

Eamonn Maguire   James Sherry   Mark Little

Ciarán O'Reilly   Stephen Maguire   Colm Bradley

SUBSTITUTES: Tom Brewster for Ciarán O'Reilly; Hughie Brady for Liam McBarron; Darragh McGrath for James Sherry

ARMAGH
Paul Hearty

Enda McNulty   Francie Bellew   Andy Mallon

Kieran Hughes   Kieran McGeeney (*Captain*)   Aidan O'Rourke

Philip Loughran   Paul McGrane

Paddy McKeever   Tony McEntee   John Toal

Steven McDonnell   Ronan Clarke   Diarmaid Marsden

SUBSTITUTES: Brian Mallon for John Toal; Andy McCann for Brian Mallon; Kevin McElvanna for Aidan O'Rourke; Oisín McConville for Paddy McKeever; Brian Mallon for Ronan Clarke

ALL-IRELAND SENIOR FOOTBALL CHAMPIONSHIP QUARTER-FINAL

DERRY VERSUS WESTMEATH
CROKE PARK
REFEREE: MICHAEL CURLEY (GALWAY)
RESULT: DERRY 2-9 WESTMEATH 0-13

SCORERS – DERRY: Enda Muldoon 1-6; Paddy Bradley 1-2; Eamonn Burke 0-1

SCORERS – WESTMEATH: Dessie Dolan 0-5; Denis Glennon 0-2; Joe Fallon 0-2; Fergal Wilson 0-2; Gary Dolan 0-1; Alan Mangan 0-1

DERRY
Barry Gillis

Kevin McGuckin   Niall McCusker   Seán Marty Lockhart (*Captain*)

Francis McEldowney   Paul McFlynn   Padraig Kelly

Fergal Doherty   Patsy Bradley

James Donaghy   Johnny McBride   Conleth Moran

Johnny Bradley   Paddy Bradley   Enda Muldoon

SUBSTITUTES: Gavin Donaghy for Conleth Moran; Eamonn Burke for Johnny Bradley; Conleith Gilligan for Johnny McBride; Gerard O'Kane for Niall McCusker

WESTMEATH
Gary Connaughton

John Keane   Damien Healy   Donal O'Donoghue

Michael Ennis   James Davitt   Derek Heavin

Rory O'Connell   David O'Shaughnessy (*Captain*)

Brian Morley   Paul Conway   Fergal Wilson

Alan Mangan   Denis Glennon   Dessie Dolan

SUBSTITUTES: Joe Fallon for Fergal Wilson; Shane Colleary for Brian Morley; Gary Dolan for Paul Conway

ALL-IRELAND SENIOR FOOTBALL CHAMPIONSHIP QUARTER-FINAL

KERRY VERSUS DUBLIN
CROKE PARK
REFEREE: PAT MCENANEY (MONAGHAN)
RESULT: KERRY 1-15 DUBLIN 1-8

SCORERS – KERRY: Dara O Cinnéide 1-5; Colm Cooper 0-5; William Kirby 0-2; Declan O'Sullivan 0-1; Liam Hassett 0-1; Paul Galvin 0-1

SCORERS – DUBLIN: Senan Connell 0-5; Jason Sherlock 1-0; Darren Homan 0-2; Conal Keaney 0-1

KERRY
Diarmuid Murphy

Tom O'Sullivan   Michael McCarthy   Aidan O'Mahony

Tomás Ó Sé   Eamon Fitzmaurice   Marc Ó Sé

Darragh Ó Sé   Paddy Kelly

Eoin Brosnan   Declan O'Sullivan   Paul Galvin

Colm Cooper   Dara Ó Cinnéide (*Captain*)   Mike Frank Russell

SUBSTITUTES: Liam Hassett for Mike Frank Russell; William Kirby for Paddy Kelly; Johnny Crowley for Declan O'Sullivan; John Sheehan for Tomás Ó Sé; Seán O'Sullivan for Aidan O'Mahony

DUBLIN
Stephen Cluxton

Barry Cahill   Paddy Christie   Paul Griffin

Paul Casey   Bryan Cullen   Shane Ryan

Darren Homan   Darren Magee

Conal Keaney   Ciarán Whelan (*Captain*)   Senan Connell

Alan Brogan   Ian Robertson   Jason Sherlock

SUBSTITUTES: Tomás Quinn for Conal Keaney; Ray Cosgrove for Ian Robertson; Jonathan Magee for Ciarán Whelan; Declan O'Mahony for Darren Homan

Paul Galvin, Kerry & Darren Magee, Dublin

Jason Sherlock, Dublin

FIRST ROUND

16th May, Páirc Uí Chaoimh:
Limerick 0-16   Tipperary 3-5

23rd May, Cusack Park:
Kerry 2-10   Clare 0-9

SEMI-FINALS

13th June, Fitzgerald Stadium:
Kerry 0-15   Cork 0-7

13th June, Gaelic Grounds:
Limerick 1-18   Waterford 0-7

FINAL

11th July, Gaelic Grounds:
Kerry 1-10   Limerick 1-10 (A Draw)

18th July, Fitzgerald Stadium:
Kerry 3-10   Limerick 2-9 (Replay)

MUNSTER SENIOR FOOTBALL CHAMPIONSHIP FIRST ROUND

LIMERICK VERSUS TIPPERARY
PÁIRC UÍ CHAOIMH (CORK)
REFEREE: MAURICE DEEGAN (LAOIS)
RESULT: LIMERICK 0-16 TIPPERARY 3-5

SCORERS – LIMERICK: Muiris Gavin 0-7; Eoin Keating 0-4; Conor Fitzgerald 0-2; Johnny Murphy 0-1; Stephen Kelly 0-1; Conor Mullane 0-1

SCORERS – TIPPERARY: Declan Browne 1-4; Aidan Fitzgerald 1-0; Paul Cahill 1-0; Glen Burke 0-1

LIMERICK
Mike Jones

Mark O'Riordan   Johnny McCarthy   Tommy Stack (*Captain*)

Conor Mullane   Stephen Lucey   Damien Reidy

John Galvin   John Quane

Stephen Kelly   Muiris Gavin   Mike O'Brien

Conor Fitzgerald   Johnny Murphy   Eoin Keating

SUBSTITUTES: Timmy Carroll for John Quane; Maurice Horan for Johnny Murphy; Micheál Reidy for Stephen Kelly

TIPPERARY
Brian Enright

Benny Hahessy   Seán Collum   Niall Curran

Robbie Costigan (*Captain*)   Damien Byrne   Glen Burke

Fergal O'Callaghan   Kevin Mulryan

Liam England   Aidan Fitzgerald   Micheál Webster

Paul Cahill   Declan Browne   Damien O'Brien

SUBSTITUTES: John Paul Looby for Micheál Webster; Patrick Halley for Liam England; Liam Cronin for Niall Curran; James Williams for Aidan Fitzgerald; David Byrne for Paul Cahill

MUNSTER SENIOR FOOTBALL CHAMPIONSHIP FIRST ROUND

KERRY VERSUS CLARE
CUSACK PARK (ENNIS)
REFEREE: GERRY KINNEAVY (ROSCOMMON) & HAULIE BEIRNE (ROSCOMMON) *
RESULT: KERRY 2-10 CLARE 0-9

SCORERS – KERRY: Eoin Brosnan 1-4; Mike Frank Russell 0-5; Johnny Crowley 1-0; Colm Cooper 0-1

SCORERS – CLARE: Denis Russell 0-3; Colm Mullen 0-2; David Russell 0-1; Odhran O'Dwyer 0-1; Evan Talty 0-1; Michael O'Dwyer 0-1

KERRY
Diarmuid Murphy

Tom O'Sullivan   Michael McCarthy   Aidan O'Mahony

Tomás Ó Sé (*Captain*)   Eamon Fitzmaurice   Seamus Moynihan

Darragh Ó Sé   William Kirby

Paul Galvin   Declan O'Sullivan   Eoin Brosnan

Colm Cooper   Johnny Crowley   Mike Frank Russell

SUBSTITUTES: Michael Quirke for Johnny Crowley; Liam Hassett for Paul Galvin; Marc Ó Sé for Tomás Ó Sé; Ronan O'Connor for Michael Quirke

CLARE
Dermot O'Brien

Padraig Gallagher   Conor Whelan   Kevin Dilleen

Noel Griffin   Brian Considine   Ronan Slattery

David Russell (Kilkee) (*Captain*)   Donal O'Sullivan

Ger Quinlan   Denis Russell   Odhran O'Dwyer

Colm Mullen   Enda Coughlan   Seán O'Meara

SUBSTITUTES: Evan Talty for Noel Griffin; Stephen Hickey for Seán O'Meara; Michael O'Shea for Odhran O'Dwyer; Michael O'Dwyer for Enda Coughlan; David Russell (Clarecastle) for Donal O'Sullivan

* Referee Gerry Kinneavy retired injured following a clash of heads with a Clare player. Haulie Beirne took charge of the game for a time and Kinneavy resumed in the second-half.

MUNSTER SENIOR FOOTBALL CHAMPIONSHIP SEMI-FINAL

KERRY VERSUS CORK
FITZGERALD STADIUM (KILLARNEY)
REFEREE: BRIAN WHITE (WEXFORD)
RESULT: KERRY 0-15 CORK 0-7

SCORERS – KERRY: Mike Frank Russell 0-7; Colm Cooper 0-3; William Kirby 0-2; Tomás Ó Sé 0-1; Eoin Brosnan 0-1; Dara Ó Cinnéide 0-1

SCORERS – CORK: Micheál Ó Cróinín 0-3; Alan Cronin 0-1; Conor McCarthy 0-1; Micheál O'Sullivan 0-1; Kevin McMahon 0-1

KERRY
Diarmuid Murphy

Tom O'Sullivan   Michael McCarthy   Aidan O'Mahony

Tomás Ó Sé (*Captain*)   Eamon Fitzmaurice   Seamus Moynihan

Darragh Ó Sé   William Kirby

Liam Hassett   Declan O'Sullivan   Eoin Brosnan

Colm Cooper   Johnny Crowley   Mike Frank Russell

SUBSTITUTES: Dara Ó Cinnéide for Johnny Crowley; Paul Galvin for Eoin Brosnan; Marc Ó Sé for Aidan O'Mahony

CORK
Kevin O'Dwyer

Seán O'Brien   Derek Kavanagh   Noel O'Leary

Eoin Sexton   Martin Cronin   Gary Murphy

Graham Canty   Dermot Hurley

Alan Cronin   Conor McCarthy   Ciarán O'Sullivan

Colin Crowley (*Captain*)   Micheál Ó Cróinín   Kevin O'Sullivan

SUBSTITUTES: Nicholas Murphy for Alan Cronin; Kevin McMahon for Ciarán O'Sullivan; Micheál O'Sullivan for Dermot Hurley; Fionán Murray for Kevin O'Sullivan

MUNSTER SENIOR FOOTBALL CHAMPIONSHIP SEMI-FINAL

LIMERICK VERSUS WATERFORD
GAELIC GROUNDS (LIMERICK)
REFEREE: THOMAS QUIGLEY (WEXFORD)
RESULT: LIMERICK 1-18 WATERFORD 0-7

SCORERS – LIMERICK: Muiris Gavin 0-8; Conor Fitzgerald 0-4; Micheál Reidy 0-3; Conor Mullane 1-0; Eoin Keating 0-1; Johnny Murphy 0-1; Damien Reidy 0-1

SCORERS – WATERFORD: Shane Walsh 0-4; Ger Power 0-2; Mick Ahearne 0-1

LIMERICK
Seamus O'Donnell

Mark O'Riordan   Johnny McCarthy   Tommy Stack (*Captain*)

Padraig Browne   Stephen Lucey   Damien Reidy

John Quane   John Galvin

Conor Mullane   Muiris Gavin   Mike O'Brien

Conor Fitzgerald   Eoin Keating   Micheál Reidy

SUBSTITUTES: Stephen Lavin for Damien Reidy; Johnny Murphy for Eoin Keating; Stephen Kelly for Conor Fitzgerald; Maurice Horan for Mike O'Brien; Mike Jones for Seamus O'Donnell

WATERFORD
Paul Hoolihan

John Moore   Edmund Rockett   Trevor Costelloe

Conan Watt   Tomás Dunphy   Niall Hennessy

Karl O'Keeffe   Andy Hubbard

John Hearne   Mick Ahearne   John Coffey

Liam Ó Lionáin   Shane Walsh   Ger Power (*Captain*)

SUBSTITUTES: Kieran Connery for Tomás Dunphy; Billy Harty for Karl O'Keeffe; Tony Whelan for Liam Ó Lionáin; Paul Ogle for John Coffey; Lee Hayes for Conan Watt

John Quane, Limerick

Johnny Crowley, Kerry

MUNSTER SENIOR FOOTBALL CHAMPIONSHIP FINAL

KERRY VERSUS LIMERICK
GAELIC GROUNDS (LIMERICK)
REFEREE: GERRY KINNEAVY (ROSCOMMON)
RESULT: KERRY 1-10 LIMERICK 1-10 (A DRAW)

SCORERS – KERRY: Mike Frank Russell 1-4; Dara Ó Cinnéide 0-3; Colm Cooper 0-2; Eoin Brosnan 0-1

SCORERS – LIMERICK: Muiris Gavin 0-4; Stephen Lavin 1-0; Conor Fitzgerald 0-2; Eoin Keating 0-2; Conor Mullane 0-1; Jason Stokes 0-1

KERRY
Diarmuid Murphy

Tom O'Sullivan   Michael McCarthy   Aidan O'Mahony

Tomás Ó Sé   Eamon Fitzmaurice   Marc Ó Sé

Darragh Ó Sé   William Kirby

Liam Hassett   Eoin Brosnan   Paul Galvin

Colm Cooper   Dara O Cinnéide (*Captain*)   Mike Frank Russell

SUBSTITUTES: Tommy Griffin for William Kirby; Johnny Crowley for Dara Ó Cinnéide; John Sheehan for Eamon Fitzmaurice

LIMERICK
Seamus O'Donnell

Mark O'Riordan   Johnny McCarthy   Tommy Stack (*Captain*)

Conor Mullane   Stephen Lucey   Stephen Lavin

Jason Stokes   John Quane

Stephen Kelly   Muiris Gavin   Mike O' Brien

Conor Fitzgerald   John Galvin   Eoin Keating

SUBSTITUTES: Johnny Murphy for Muiris Gavin; Damien Reidy for Stephen Lavin

MUNSTER SENIOR FOOTBALL CHAMPIONSHIP FINAL REPLAY

KERRY VERSUS LIMERICK
FITZGERALD STADIUM (KILLARNEY)
REFEREE: MICHAEL CURLEY (GALWAY)
RESULT: KERRY 3-10 LIMERICK 2-9

SCORERS – KERRY: Dara Ó Cinnéide 1-7; Eoin Brosnan 1-1; Tomás Ó Sé 1-0;
Mike Frank Russell 0-1; Paul Galvin 0-1

SCORERS – LIMERICK: Muiris Gavin 0-5; Eoin Keating 1-1; Stephen Kelly 1-0;
John Galvin 0-1; John Quane 0-1; Conor Fitzgerald 0-1

KERRY
Diarmuid Murphy
Tom O'Sullivan　　Michael McCarthy　　Aidan O'Mahony
Tomás Ó Sé　　Eamon Fitzmaurice　　Marc Ó Sé
Darragh Ó Sé　　Eoin Brosnan
Liam Hassett　　Dara O Cinnéide (*Captain*)　　Paul Galvin
Colm Cooper　　Johnny Crowley　　Mike Frank Russell

SUBSTITUTES: Tommy Griffin for Johnny Crowley; William Kirby for Liam Hassett;
Seán Ó Sullivan for Paul Galvin; Declan Quill for Colm Cooper

LIMERICK
Seamus O'Donnell
Mark O'Riordan　　Johnny McCarthy　　Tommy Stack (*Captain*)
Conor Mullane　　Stephen Lucey　　Stephen Lavin
John Quane　　Jason Stokes
Mike O' Brien　　Muiris Gavin　　Eoin Keating
Stephen Kelly　　John Galvin　　Conor Fitzgerald

SUBSTITUTES: Damien Reidy for Mike O'Brien; Johnny Murphy for John Quane

Muiris Gavin, Limerick

FIRST ROUND

2nd May, Gaelic Park:
Mayo 3-28   New York 1-8

23rd May, Dr. Hyde Park:
Roscommon 1-10   Sligo 0-13   (A Draw)

29th May, Markievicz Park: (Replay)
Roscommon 2-16   Sligo 1-15   (After Extra-time)

30th May, Ruislip:
Galway 8-14   London 0-8

SEMI-FINALS

20th June, Páirc Seán Mhic Diarmada:
Roscommon 0-13   Leitrim 1-10   (A Draw)

26th June, Dr. Hyde Park:
Roscommon 1-9   Leitrim 0-5   (Replay)

27th June, McHale Park:
Mayo 0-18   Galway 1-9

FINAL

18th July, McHale Park:
Mayo 2-13   Roscommon 0-9

CONNACHT SENIOR FOOTBALL CHAMPIONSHIP FIRST ROUND

MAYO VERSUS NEW YORK
GAELIC PARK (NEW YORK)
REFEREE: MICHAEL COLLINS (CORK)
RESULT: MAYO 3-28 NEW YORK 1-8

SCORERS – MAYO: Conor Mortimer 1-12; Austin O'Malley 1-3; Andy Moran 0-5; Michael Moyles 1-1; James Gill 0-2; Marty McNicholas 0-2; Alan Dillon 0-1; Fergal Costello 0-1; Brian Maloney 0-1

SCORERS – NEW YORK: Kenny O'Connor 1-1; Kevin Lilly 0-3; Eric Bradley 0-2; Mark Dobbin 0-2

MAYO
Peter Burke

Dermot Geraghty   Pat Kelly   Gary Ruane

Fergal Costello (*Captain*)   Declan Sweeney   James Nallen

David Heaney   David Brady

James Gill   Alan Dillon   Andy Moran

Conor Mortimer   Brian Maloney   Marty McNicholas

SUBSTITUTES: Austin O'Malley for Brian Maloney; Ronan McGarrity for David Heaney; Michael Moyles for Alan Dillon; Peadar Gardiner for James Nallen; Gary Mullins for Fergal Costello

NEW YORK
Eunan Doherty

Dermot Costello   Paul O'Connor   Pa Murphy

Martin Slowey   Kevin Newell   David Callaghan

Ken O'Connor   Jason Killeen (*Captain*)

Shane McInerney   Eric Bradley   Bingo O'Driscoll

Kevin Lilly   Shane Russell   Brian Newman

SUBSTITUTES: Gary Dowd for Shane McInerney; Jamie Shaw for David Callaghan; Paul Higgins for Shane Russell; Mark Dobbin for Bingo O'Driscoll; Michael Keaveney for Brian Newman

CONNACHT SENIOR FOOTBALL CHAMPIONSHIP FIRST ROUND

ROSCOMMON VERSUS SLIGO
DR HYDE PARK (ROSCOMMON)
REFEREE: JOE MCQUILLAN (CAVAN)
RESULT: ROSCOMMON 1-10 SLIGO 0-13 (A DRAW)

SCORERS – ROSCOMMON: Frankie Dolan 0-6; Karol Mannion 1-2;
Seamus O'Neill 0-1; Nigel Dineen 0-1

SCORERS – SLIGO: Dessie Sloyan 0-5; Gerry McGowan 0-3; Seán Davey 0-2;
Mark Brehony 0-2; Michael McNamara 0-1

ROSCOMMON
Shane Curran (*Captain*)

John Whyte	Michael Ryan	John Nolan
David Casey	Francie Grehan	John Rogers
Seamus O'Neill	Stephen Lohan	
Gary Cox	Nigel Dineen	Derek Connellan
Ger Heneghan	Karol Mannion	Frankie Dolan

SUBSTITUTES: Paul Noone for David Casey; John Tiernan for Derek Connellan;
Jarlath Egan for Ger Heneghan; Brian Higgins for Stephen Lohan

SLIGO
Philip Greene

Noel McGuire	Patrick Naughton	Brendan Phillips
Johnny Martyn	Michael Langan	Philip Gallagher
Gary Maye	Seán Davey	
Kieran Quinn	Mark Brehony	Eamonn O'Hara (*Captain*)
Dessie Sloyan	Michael McNamara	Gerry McGowan

SUBSTITUTES: Padraic Doohan for Philip Gallagher; Brian Curran for Kieran Quinn;
Philip Neary for Gary Maye; Jonathan Davey for Gerry McGowan

CONNACHT SENIOR FOOTBALL CHAMPIONSHIP
FIRST ROUND REPLAY

ROSCOMMON VERSUS SLIGO
MARKIEVICZ PARK (SLIGO)
REFEREE: AIDAN MANGAN (KERRY)
RESULT: ROSCOMMON 2-16 SLIGO 1-15 (AFTER EXTRA-TIME)

SCORERS – ROSCOMMON: Shane Curran 1-1; Ger Heneghan 1-1; Frankie Dolan 0-3; Karol Mannion 0-2; Seamus O'Neill 0-2; Francie Grehan 0-2; Paul Noone 0-1; Andy McPadden 0-1; Gary Cox 0-1; John Tiernan 0-1; Jonathan Dunning 0-1

SCORERS – SLIGO: Paul Taylor 1-4; Dessie Sloyan 0-4; Seán Davey 0-3; Mark Brehony 0-2; Michael McNamara 0-1; Jonathan Davey 0-1

ROSCOMMON
Shane Curran (*Captain*)

John Whyte	Michael Ryan	John Nolan
Paul Noone	Francie Grehan	John Rogers
Seamus O'Neill	Stephen Lohan	
Gary Cox	Nigel Dineen	Brian Higgins
Ger Heneghan	Karol Mannion	Frankie Dolan

SUBSTITUTES: Derek Connellan for Brian Higgins; Andy McPadden for John Rogers; Jonathan Dunning for Ger Heneghan; David Casey for Nigel Dineen; Eamonn Towey for Paul Noone; John Tiernan for Derek Connellan

Frankie Dolan was sent-off in normal time –
Ger Heneghan came on in extra-time to bring Roscommon back to fifteen players

SLIGO
Philip Greene

Johnny Martyn	Noel McGuire	Brendan Phillips
David Durkin	Michael Langan	Padraic Doohan
Eamonn O'Hara (*Captain*)		Seán Davey
Brian Curran	Mark Brehony	Michael McNamara
Dessie Sloyan	Paul Taylor	Gerry McGowan

SUBSTITUTES: Dara McGarty for Brian Curran; Jonathan Davey for David Durkin; Kieran Quinn for Gerry McGowan; Paul Durcan for Michael McNamara; Adrian Marren for Eamonn O'Hara

CONNACHT SENIOR FOOTBALL CHAMPIONSHIP FIRST ROUND

GALWAY VERSUS LONDON
RUISLIP (LONDON)
REFEREE: JIM WHITE (DONEGAL)
RESULT: GALWAY 8-14 LONDON 0-8

SCORERS – GALWAY: Padraic Joyce 2-3; Joe Bergin 2-1; Michael Donnellan 2-1; Nicky Joyce 0-3; John Devane 0-3; Michael Meehan 1-0; Tommie Joyce 1-0; Matthew Clancy 0-1; Seán Óg de Paor 0-1; Seán Ó Domhnaill 0-1

SCORERS – LONDON: Scott Doran 0-3; Fergus McMahon 0-2; Gary Kane 0-1; Gordon Weldon 0-1; Darragh Kinneavy 0-1

GALWAY
Brian O'Donoghue
Barry Dooney   Kieran Fitzgerald   Clive Monaghan
Declan Meehan (*Captain*)   Paul Clancy   Seán Óg de Paor
Joe Bergin   Seán Ó Domhnaill
Tommie Joyce   Michael Donnellan   John Devane
Michael Meehan   Padraic Joyce   Nickey Joyce

SUBSTITUTES: Matthew Clancy for Tommie Joyce; Derek Savage for John Devane; Michael Comer for Clive Monaghan; Noel Meehan for Michael Donnellan; Damien Burke for Seán Óg de Paor

LONDON
Gavin McEvoy
Charles Harrisson   Damien McKenna   Seán Murphy
Aidan McLarnon   Johnny Niblock (*Captain*)   Karl Scanlon
Gary Kane   Paddy Quinn
Scott Doran   Fergus McMahon   Brendan Egan
Patrick Lynott   Darragh Kinneavy   Barry McDonagh

SUBSTITUTES: Gordon Weldon for Barry McDonagh; Seamus Byrnes for Patrick Lynott; Morgan Drea for Seán Murphy; Michael Lillis for Gavin McEvoy; Teu Ó hAilpín for Seamus Byrnes

Padraic Joyce, Galway

CONNACHT SENIOR FOOTBALL CHAMPIONSHIP SEMI-FINAL

ROSCOMMON VERSUS LEITRIM
PÁIRC SEÁN MHIC DIARMADA (CARRICK-ON-SHANNON)
REFEREE: MICHAEL HUGHES (TYRONE)
RESULT: ROSCOMMON 0-13 LEITRIM 1-10 (A DRAW)

SCORERS – ROSCOMMON: Frankie Dolan 0-6; Seamus O'Neill 0-3;
Francie Grehan 0-2; Gary Cox 0-1; Stephen Lohan 0-1

SCORERS – LEITRIM: Michael Foley 1-1; Colin Regan 0-2; Barry Prior 0-1;
Declan Maxwell 0-1; John McKeon 0-1; Johnny Goldrick 0-1; Fintan McBrien 0-1;
Shane Canning 0-1; Pat Farrell 0-1

ROSCOMMON
Shane Curran (*Captain*)

John Whyte	Michael Ryan	John Nolan
David Casey	Francie Grehan	Andy McPadden
Seamus O'Neill		Stephen Lohan
Brian Higgins	Frankie Dolan	Gary Cox
Nigel Dineen	Karol Mannion	Ger Heneghan

SUBSTITUTES: John Rogers for Andy McPadden; Jonathan Dunning for Nigel Dineen;
John Tiernan for Brian Higgins; Eamonn Towey for Ger Heneghan

LEITRIM
Gareth Phelan

Dermot Reynolds	Seamus Quinn	Michael McGuinness
Niall Gilbane	John McKeon	Barry Prior
Declan Maxwell	Chris Carroll (*Captain*)	
Johnny Goldrick	Fintan McBrien	Colin Regan
Donal Brennan	Jimmy Guckian	Michael Foley

SUBSTITUTES: Shane Canning for Jimmy Guckian; James Clancy for Donal Brennan;
Pat Farrell for Johnny Goldrick; Noel Doonan for Fintan McBrien

CONNACHT SENIOR FOOTBALL CHAMPIONSHIP
SEMI-FINAL REPLAY

ROSCOMMON VERSUS LEITRIM
DR. HYDE PARK (ROSCOMMON)
REFEREE: JOHN GEANEY (CORK)
RESULT: ROSCOMMON 1-9 LEITRIM 0-5

SCORERS – ROSCOMMON: John Hanly 1-1; Frankie Dolan 0-3; John Tiernan 0-2; Gary Cox 0-2; Jonathan Dunning 0-1

SCORERS – LEITRIM: Michael Foley 0-2; Fintan McBrien 0-1; Johnny Goldrick 0-1; Jimmy Guckian 0-1

ROSCOMMON
Shane Curran (*Captain*)

John Whyte	Michael Ryan	John Nolan
Eamonn Towey	Francie Grehan	David Casey
Seamus O'Neill	Stephen Lohan	
Derek Connellan	John Hanly	Gary Cox
Ger Heneghan	Karol Mannion	Frankie Dolan

SUBSTITUTES: Jonathan Dunning for Ger Heneghan; John Tiernan for Derek Connellan; John Rogers for David Casey; Brian Higgins for Gary Cox; David O'Connor for John Hanly

LEITRIM
Gareth Phelan

Dermot Reynolds	Seamus Quinn	Michael McGuinness
Niall Gilbane	John McKeon	Barry Prior
Declan Maxwell	Chris Carroll (*Captain*)	
Johnny Goldrick	Jimmy Guckian	Colin Regan
Donal Brennan	Fintan McBrien	Michael Foley

SUBSTITUTES: Shane Canning for Declan Maxwell; Pat Farrell for Donal Brennan; Dermot Kennedy for Johnny Goldrick; Donnacha Lynch for Niall Gilbane; Brendan Brennan for Fintan McBrien

CONNACHT SENIOR FOOTBALL CHAMPIONSHIP SEMI-FINAL

MAYO VERSUS GALWAY
MCHALE PARK (CASTLEBAR)
REFEREE: DAVID COLDRICK (MEATH)
RESULT: MAYO 0-18   GALWAY 1-9

SCORERS – MAYO: Conor Mortimer 0-8; Ciarán McDonald 0-3; James Gill 0-2; Brian Maloney 0-2; David Heaney 0-1; Trevor Mortimer 0-1; Ronan McGarrity 0-1

SCORERS – GALWAY: Padraic Joyce 0-5; Michael Meehan 1-1; Michael Donnellan 0-3

MAYO
Fintan Ruddy

Conor Moran   David Heaney   Gary Ruane

Gary Mullins   James Nallen   Fergal Costello (*Captain*)

James Gill   Ronan McGarrity

Marty McNicholas   Ciarán McDonald   Alan Dillon

Conor Mortimer   Trevor Mortimer   Brian Maloney

SUBSTITUTES: Peadar Gardiner for Fergal Costello;
David Brady for Marty McNicholas; Andy Moran for Trevor Mortimer;
Pat Kelly for Gary Mullins

GALWAY
Brian O'Donoghue

Michael Comer   Kieran Fitzgerald   Barry Dooney

Declan Meehan (*Captain*)   Paul Clancy   Tomás Meehan

Joe Bergin   Seán Ó Domhnaill

Michael Meehan   Michael Donnellan   Matthew Clancy

Derek Savage   Padraic Joyce   Tommie Joyce

SUBSTITUTES: Damien Burke for Michael Comer; Kevin Walsh for Tommie Joyce;
Gary Fahey for Barry Dooney; John Devane for Seán Ó Domhnaill

Ronan McGarrity, Mayo

Gary Cox, Roscommon

CONNACHT SENIOR FOOTBALL CHAMPIONSHIP FINAL

MAYO VERSUS ROSCOMMON
MCHALE PARK (CASTLEBAR)
REFEREE: BRIAN WHITE (WEXFORD)
RESULT: MAYO 2-13 ROSCOMMON 0-9

SCORERS – MAYO: Conor Mortimer 0-9; Trevor Mortimer 1-1; Austin O'Malley 1-0; Ciarán McDonald 0-1; Conor Moran 0-1; Alan Dillon 0-1

SCORERS – ROSCOMMON: Ger Heneghan 0-5; Stephen Lohan 0-1; John Hanly 0-1; Frankie Dolan 0-1; Nigel Dineen 0-1

MAYO
Fintan Ruddy
Conor Moran   David Heaney   Gary Ruane
Gary Mullins   James Nallen   Fergal Costello (*Captain*)
David Brady   Ronan McGarrity
James Gill   Ciarán McDonald   Alan Dillon
Conor Mortimer   Trevor Mortimer   Brian Maloney

SUBSTITUTES: Peadar Gardiner for Gary Mullins; Pat Kelly for Fergal Costello; Andy Moran for Alan Dillon; Austin O'Malley for Brian Maloney; Declan Sweeney for Conor Moran

ROSCOMMON
Shane Curran (*Captain*)
John Whyte   Michael Ryan   John Nolan
David Casey   Francie Grehan   Andy McPadden
Seamus O'Neill   Stephen Lohan
Gary Cox   John Hanly   John Tiernan
Jonathan Dunning   Karol Mannion   Frankie Dolan

SUBSTITUTES: Ger Heneghan for Frankie Dolan; Nigel Dineen for John Hanly; John Rogers for John Nolan; Derek Connellan for Jonathan Dunning; Ray Cox for John Tiernan

FIRST ROUND

9th May, St. Tighearnach's Park:
Tyrone 1-17   Derry 1-6

QUARTER-FINALS

16th May, Casement Park:
Cavan 1-13   Down 1-13 (A Draw)

23rd May, St. Tighearnach's Park:
Armagh 2-19   Monaghan 0-10

29th May, Kingspan Breffni Park:
Cavan 3-13   Down 2-12 (Replay)

30th May, MacCumhaill Park:
Donegal 1-15   Antrim 1-9

6th June, St. Tighearnach's Park:
Tyrone 1-13   Fermanagh 0-12

SEMI-FINALS
13th June, St. Tighearnach's Park:
Armagh 0-13   Cavan 0-11

20th June, St. Tighearnach's Park
Donegal 1-11   Tyrone 0-9

FINAL

11th July, Croke Park:
Armagh 3-15   Donegal 0-11

ULSTER SENIOR FOOTBALL CHAMPIONSHIP FIRST ROUND

TYRONE VERSUS DERRY
ST. TIGHEARNACH'S PARK (CLONES)
REFEREE: BRIAN WHITE (WEXFORD)
RESULT: TYRONE 1-17 DERRY 1-6

SCORERS – TYRONE: Kevin Hughes 1-2; Mark Harte 0-4; Seán Cavanagh 0-4;
Brian Dooher 0-2; Colm McCullagh 0-2; Stephen O'Neill 0-1; Philip Jordan 0-1;
Enda McGinley 0-1

SCORERS – DERRY: Paddy Bradley 0-4; Padraig Kelly 1-0; Enda Muldoon 0-1;
Francis McEldowney 0-1

TYRONE
John Devine
Ryan McMenamin   Conor Gormley   Ciarán Gourley
Brendan Donnelly   Gavin Devlin   Philip Jordan
Colin Holmes   Seán Cavanagh
Brian Dooher (*Captain*)   Brian McGuigan   Enda McGinley
Mark Harte   Kevin Hughes   Colm McCullagh

SUBSTITUTES: Joe McMahon for Brendan Donnelly; Stephen O'Neill for Brian Dooher

DERRY
Barry Gillis
Seán Marty Lockhart (*Captain*)   Niall McCusker   Padraig Kelly
Padraig O'Kane   Kevin McGuckin   Francis McEldowney
Fergal Doherty   Enda Muldoon
Patsy Bradley   Conleith Gilligan   Johnny McBride
Jim Kelly   Paddy Bradley   Paul McFlynn

SUBSTITUTES: Ryan Lynch for Paul McFlynn; James Donaghy for Jim Kelly;
Johnny Bradley for Patsy Bradley

ULSTER SENIOR FOOTBALL CHAMPIONSHIP QUARTER-FINAL

CAVAN VERSUS DOWN
CASEMENT PARK (BELFAST)
REFEREE: DAVID COLDRICK (MEATH)
RESULT: CAVAN 1-13 DOWN 1-13 (A DRAW)

SCORERS – CAVAN: Mícheál Lyng 0-6; Jason O'Reilly 1-2; Gerald Pierson 0-3; Larry Reilly 0-1; Seánie Johnston 0-1

SCORERS – DOWN: Benny Coulter 1-2; Liam Doyle 0-4; Daniel Hughes 0-4; John Clarke 0-1; Ronan Sexton 0-1; Aidan O'Prey 0-1

CAVAN
Eoghan Elliott

Eamonn Reilly   Darren Rabbitte   Paul Brady

Anthony Forde   Trevor Crowe   Anthony Gaynor

Pearse McKenna   Cathal Collins

Larry Reilly (*Captain*)   Mícheál Lyng   Mark McKeever

Gerald Pierson   Jason O'Reilly   Seánie Johnston

SUBSTITUTES: Karl Crotty for Cathal Collins; Peter Reilly for Seánie Johnston

DOWN
Mickey McVeigh

Michael Higgins   Alan Molloy   Adrian Scullion

John Clarke   Martin Cole   Seán Farrell

Dan Gordon   Gregory McCartan (*Captain*)

Liam Doyle   Shane Ward   Ronan Sexton

Eoin McCartan   Benny Coulter   Daniel Hughes

SUBSTITUTES: John Lavery for Seán Farrell; Colin McCrickard for Gregory McCartan; Brendan Grant for Ronan Sexton; Aidan O'Prey for Eoin McCartan

ULSTER SENIOR FOOTBALL CHAMPIONSHIP QUARTER-FINAL

ARMAGH VERSUS MONAGHAN
ST. TIGHEARNACH'S PARK (CLONES)
REFEREE: JOHN BANNON (LONGFORD)
RESULT: ARMAGH 2-19 MONAGHAN 0-10

SCORERS – ARMAGH: Steven McDonnell 1-5; Oisín McConville 0-5; Ronan Clarke 1-2; Paddy McKeever 0-4; Tony McEntee 0-1; Martin O'Rourke 0-1; Brian Mallon 0-1

SCORERS – MONAGHAN: Paul Finlay 0-4; Dick Clerkin 0-2; Damien Freeman 0-2; Rory Woods 0-2

ARMAGH
Paul Hearty

| Enda McNulty | Francie Bellew | Andy McCann |
| Aidan O'Rourke | Andy Mallon | Kieran Hughes |

Philip Loughran   Paul McGrane (*Captain*)

| Paddy McKeever | Tony McEntee | Oisín McConville |
| Steven McDonnell | Ronan Clarke | Martin O'Rourke |

SUBSTITUTES: Brian Mallon for Ronan Clarke; Kevin McElvanna for Andy McCann; Paul McCormack for Enda McNulty; Stephen Kernan for Martin O'Rourke

MONAGHAN
Glenn Murphy

| Edmund Lennon | James Coyle | Vincent Corey |
| Gary McQuaid | Dermot Duffy (*Captain*) | Dessie Mone |

Jason Hughes   Eoin Lennon

| Paul Finlay | Thomas Freeman | Dick Clerkin |
| Kieran Tavey | Raymond Ronaghan | Damien Freeman |

SUBSTITUTES: Rory Woods for Kieran Tavey; John Paul Mone for Vincent Corey; Dermot McDermott for Edmund Lennon; James Conlon for Jason Hughes; Nicholas Corrigan for Raymond Ronaghan

ULSTER SENIOR FOOTBALL CHAMPIONSHIP
QUARTER-FINAL REPLAY

CAVAN VERSUS DOWN
KINGSPAN BREFFNI PARK (CAVAN)
REFEREE: SEAMUS MCCORMACK (MEATH)
RESULT: CAVAN 3-13 DOWN 2-12

SCORERS – CAVAN: Jason O'Reilly 1-3; Micheál Lyng 0-5; Mark McKeever 0-3; Peter Reilly 1-0; Dermot McCabe 1-0; Trevor Crowe 0-1; Pearse McKenna 0-1

SCORERS – DOWN: Benny Coulter 2-2; Gregory McCartan 0-3; Aidan O'Prey 0-3; Daniel Hughes 0-2; Dan Gordon 0-1; Ronan Murtagh 0-1

CAVAN
Eoghan Elliott
Eamonn Reilly   Darren Rabbitte   Paul Brady
Karl Crotty   Anthony Gaynor   Anthony Forde
Pearse McKenna   Trevor Crowe
Larry Reilly (*Captain*)   Micheál Lyng   Mark McKeever
Gerald Pierson   Jason O'Reilly   Seánie Johnston

SUBSTITUTES: Cathal Collins for Eamonn Reilly; Dermot McCabe for Gerald Pierson; Peter Reilly for Seánie Johnston; Rory Donohoe for Paul Brady; Seán Brady for Mark McKeever

DOWN
Mickey McVeigh
Brendan Grant   Alan Molloy   Adrian Scullion
John Clarke   Martin Cole   Seán Farrell
Gregory McCartan (*Captain*)   Dan Gordon
Eoin McCartan   Shane Ward   Ronan Sexton
Benny Coulter   Aidan O'Prey   Daniel Hughes

SUBSTITUTES: Ronan Murtagh for Shane Ward; Ambrose Rodgers for Ronan Sexton; John Lavery for Eoin McCartan

ULSTER SENIOR FOOTBALL CHAMPIONSHIP QUARTER-FINAL

DONEGAL VERSUS ANTRIM
MACCUMHAILL PARK (BALLYBOFEY)
REFEREE: PAT FOX (WESTMEATH)
RESULT: DONEGAL 1-15 ANTRIM 1-9

SCORERS – DONEGAL: Adrian Sweeney 0-5; Brendan Devenney 0-3;
Colm McFadden 0-3; Michael Hegarty 0-3; Brendan Boyle 1-0; Christy Toye 0-1

SCORERS – ANTRIM: Kevin Madden 0-6; Darren O'Hare 1-1; James Marron 0-1;
Kevin McGourty 0-1

DONEGAL
Paul Durcan
Niall McCready   Raymond Sweeney   Damien Diver
Eamonn McGee   Barry Monaghan   Kevin Cassidy
Brendan Boyle   Brian McLaughlin
Christy Toye   Michael Hegarty   Stephen McDermott
Colm McFadden   Adrian Sweeney (*Captain*)   Brendan Devenney

SUBSTITUTES: Paul McGonigle for Brian McLaughlin; Karl Lacey for Niall McCready;
Shane Carr for Eamonn McGee; Brian Roper for Christy Toye

ANTRIM
Seán McGreevy
Niall Ward   Colin Brady   Tony Convery
Gearóid Adams   Seán Kelly   Anto Finnegan
Joe Quinn   Mark McCrory
Martin McCarry   Kevin Brady (*Captain*)   Kevin McGourty
Paul Doherty   Darren O'Hare   Kevin Madden

SUBSTITUTES: Mark Dougan for Mark McCrory; James Marron for Paul Doherty;
John McKeever for Niall Ward; Kevin Murray for Gearóid Adams

SUNDAY, JUNE 6, 2004

ULSTER SENIOR FOOTBALL CHAMPIONSHIP QUARTER-FINAL

TYRONE VERSUS FERMANAGH
ST. TIGHEARNACH'S PARK (CLONES)
REFEREE: SEAMUS MCCORMACK (MEATH)
RESULT: TYRONE 1-13 FERMANAGH 0-12

SCORERS – TYRONE: Owen Mulligan 0-5; Mark Harte 1-2; Kevin Hughes 0-2;
Seán Cavanagh 0-1; Ciarán Gourley 0-1; Stephen O'Neill 0-1; Brian McGuigan 0-1

SCORERS – FERMANAGH: Stephen Maguire 0-5; Marty McGrath 0-2;
James Sherry 0-2; Damien Kelly 0-1; Mark Little 0-1; Eamonn Maguire 0-1

TYRONE
John Devine
Ryan McMenamin (*Captain*)   Conor Gormley   Ciarán Gourley
Joe McMahon   Gavin Devlin   Philip Jordan
Colin Holmes   Seán Cavanagh
Owen Mulligan   Brian McGuigan   Stephen O'Neill
Mark Harte   Kevin Hughes   Colm McCullagh

SUBSTITUTES: Ger Cavlan for Colm McCullagh; Michael Coleman for Colin Holmes

FERMANAGH
Niall Tinney
Niall Bogue   Barry Owens   Hughie Brady
Raymond Johnston   Shane McDermott (*Captain*)   Damien Kelly
Marty McGrath   Liam McBarron
Eamonn Maguire   James Sherry   Mark Little
Ciarán O'Reilly   Stephen Maguire   Colm Bradley

SUBSTITUTES: Peter Sherry for Barry Owens; Mark Murphy for Ciarán O'Reilly;
Darragh McGrath for Colm Bradley

yan McMenamin, Tyrone

Stephen O'Neill, Tyror

ULSTER SENIOR FOOTBALL CHAMPIONSHIP SEMI-FINAL

ARMAGH VERSUS CAVAN
ST. TIGHEARNACH'S PARK (CLONES)
REFEREE: MICHAEL MONAHAN (KILDARE)
RESULT: ARMAGH 0-13   CAVAN 0-11

SCORERS – ARMAGH: Oisín McConville 0-5; Steven McDonnell 0-2; Brian Mallon 0-2; Paddy McKeever 0-1; Ronan Clarke 0-1; Diarmaid Marsden 0-1; Kevin McElvanna 0-1

SCORERS – CAVAN: Micheál Lyng 0-4; Gerald Pearson 0-3; Larry Reilly 0-3; Dermot McCabe 0-1

ARMAGH
Paul Hearty

Enda McNulty	Francie Bellew	Andy Mallon
Kieran Hughes	Aidan O'Rourke	Andy McCann
John Toal	Paul McGrane (*Captain*)	
Paddy McKeever	Tony McEntee	Oisín McConville
Steven McDonnell	Ronan Clarke	Martin O'Rourke

SUBSTITUTES: Kevin McElvanna for Andy Mallon;
Diarmaid Marsden for Tony McEntee; Kieran McGeeney for Andy McCann;
Brian Mallon for Ronan Clarke

CAVAN
Eoghan Elliott

Cathal Collins	Darren Rabbitte	Rory Donohoe
Anthony Forde	Anthony Gaynor	Karl Crotty
Pearse McKenna	Trevor Crowe	
Larry Reilly (*Captain*)	Micheál Lyng	Mark McKeever
Jason O'Reilly	Peter Reilly	Gerald Pearson

SUBSTITUTES: Dermot McCabe for Peter Reilly; Michael Brides for Rory Donohoe;
Shane Cole for Trevor Crowe; Seánie Johnston for Jason O'Reilly

ULSTER SENIOR FOOTBALL CHAMPIONSHIP SEMI-FINAL

DONEGAL VERSUS TYRONE
ST. TIGHEARNACH'S PARK (CLONES)
REFEREE: GERRY KINNEAVY (ROSCOMMON)
RESULT: DONEGAL 1-11 TYRONE 0-9

SCORERS – DONEGAL: Colm McFadden 1-7; Adrian Sweeney 0-1; Brian Roper 0-1; Barry Monaghan 0-1; Christy Toye 0-1

SCORERS – TYRONE: Owen Mulligan 0-3; Stephen O'Neill 0-2; Mark Harte 0-1; Shane Sweeney 0-1; Brian McGuigan 0-1; Joe McMahon 0-1

DONEGAL
Paul Durcan

Niall McCready   Raymond Sweeney   Damien Diver

Eamonn McGee   Barry Monaghan   Shane Carr

Brendan Boyle   Brian McLaughlin

Christy Toye   Michael Hegarty   Brian Roper

Colm McFadden   Adrian Sweeney (*Captain*)   Brendan Devenney

SUBSTITUTES: Stephen McDermott for Brian McLaughlin; Stephen Cassidy for Brendan Devenney; John Gildea for Christy Toye

TYRONE
John Devine

Ryan McMenamin   Conor Gormley   Ciarán Gourley

Joe McMahon   Shane Sweeney   Philip Jordan

Ger Cavlan   Seán Cavanagh

Brian Dooher (*Captain*)   Brian McGuigan   Stephen O'Neill

Mark Harte   Kevin Hughes   Owen Mulligan

SUBSTITUTES: Enda McGinley for Mark Harte; Michael McGee for Ciarán Gourley; Colin Holmes for Kevin Hughes

ULSTER SENIOR FOOTBALL CHAMPIONSHIP FINAL

ARMAGH VERSUS DONEGAL
CROKE PARK
REFEREE: MICHAEL COLLINS (CORK)
RESULT: ARMAGH 3-15 DONEGAL 0-11

SCORERS – ARMAGH: Oisín McConville 1-3; Paddy McKeever 1-3;
Diarmaid Marsden 1-2; Tony McEntee 0-2; Steven McDonnell 0-2; Brian Mallon 0-1;
Ronan Clarke 0-1; Philip Loughran 0-1

SCORERS – DONEGAL: Colm McFadden 0-4; Brendan Devenney 0-2;
Adrian Sweeney 0-1; Brian Roper 0-1; Michael Hegarty 0-1; John Gildea 0-1;
Rory Kavanagh 0-1

ARMAGH
Paul Hearty

Enda McNulty   Francie Bellew   Andy Mallon

Kieran Hughes   Kieran McGeeney (*Captain*)   Aidan O'Rourke

Philip Loughran   Paul McGrane

Paddy McKeever   Tony McEntee   Oisín McConville

Steven McDonnell   Ronan Clarke   Diarmaid Marsden

SUBSTITUTES: Brian Mallon for Ronan Clarke; John Toal for Philip Loughran;
Andy McCann for Kieran McGeeney; Justin McNulty for Francie Bellew;
John McEntee for Diarmaid Marsden

DONEGAL
Paul Durcan

Niall McCready   Raymond Sweeney   Damien Diver

Eamonn McGee   Barry Monaghan   Shane Carr

Brendan Boyle   Stephen McDermott

Christy Toye   Michael Hegarty   Brian Roper

Colm McFadden   Adrian Sweeney (*Captain*)   Brendan Devenney

SUBSTITUTES: John Gildea for Stephen McDermott; Rory Kavanagh for Christy Toye;
Paul McGonigle for Brian Roper; John Haran for Adrian Sweeney;
Karl Lacey for Eamonn McGee

Eamonn Maguire, Fermanagh

Enda Muldoon, Derry

FIRST ROUND

9th May, O'Connor Park:
Carlow 4-15   Longford 1-16

16th May, Parnell Park:
Wexford 2-10   Louth 0-8

23rd May, Croke Park:
Westmeath 0-11   Offaly 0-10

23rd May, Croke Park:
Meath 2-13   Wicklow 1-8

30th May, Dr Cullen Park:
Laois 0-15   Carlow 1-7

QUARTER-FINALS

6th June, Croke Park:
Westmeath 0-14   Dublin 0-12

6th June, Croke Park:
Wexford 0-12   Kildare 0-10

SEMI-FINALS

20th June, Croke Park:
Laois 1-13   Meath 0-9

27th June, Croke Park:
Westmeath 2-15   Wexford 1-14

FINAL

18th July, Croke Park
Westmeath 0-13 Laois 0-13 (A Draw)

FINAL REPLAY

24th July, Croke Park
Westmeath 0-12   Laois 0-10

Brian 'Beano' McDonald, Laois

Paul McDonald, Laois & Johnny Nevin, Carlo

LEINSTER SENIOR FOOTBALL CHAMPIONSHIP FIRST ROUND

CARLOW VERSUS LONGFORD
O'CONNOR PARK (TULLAMORE)
REFEREE: THOMAS QUIGLEY (WEXFORD)
RESULT: CARLOW 4-15 LONGFORD 1-16

SCORERS - CARLOW: Simon Rea 2-3; Patrick Hickey 1-1; Mark Carpenter 1-1; Seán Kavanagh 0-3; Johnny Nevin 0-2; John Hayden 0-1; Joe Byrne 0-1; Brian Carbery 0-1; Thomas Walsh 0-1; Brian Kelly 0-1

SCORERS - LONGFORD: Padraic Davis 1-6; Paul Barden 0-4; Niall Sheridan 0-3; Trevor Smullen 0-1; Liam Keenan 0-1; Jamesie Martin 0-1

CARLOW
James Clarke
Brian Farrell   Stephen O'Brien   Cormac McCarthy
Ken Walker   John Hayden   Joe Byrne
Mark Brennan   Thomas Walsh
Patrick Hickey   Johnny Nevin   Mark Carpenter (*Captain*)
Simon Rea   Seán Kavanagh   Brian Carbery

SUBSTITUTES: Barry English for Ken Walker; Brian Kelly for Brian Carbery; Willie Power for Mark Brennan

LONGFORD
Gavin Tonra
Donal Ledwith   Cathal Conefrey   Shane Carroll
Enda Ledwith   David Hannify   Arthur O'Connor
Liam Keenan   Trevor Smullen
Paul O'Hara   John Kenny   Paul Barden (*Captain*)
Jamesie Martin   Niall Sheridan   Padraic Davis

SUBSTITUTES: Stephen Lynch for John Kenny; Mark Lennon for Jamesie Martin; Michael Kelly for Stephen Lynch

Ollie McDonnell, Lout

LEINSTER SENIOR FOOTBALL CHAMPIONSHIP FIRST ROUND

WEXFORD VERSUS LOUTH
PARNELL PARK (DUBLIN)
REFEREE: MICHAEL HUGHES (TYRONE)
RESULT: WEXFORD 2-10 LOUTH 0-8

SCORERS – WEXFORD: Matty Forde 0-8; John Hegarty 1-0; Darren Foran 1-0; Paddy Colfer 0-1; George Sunderland 0-1

SCORERS – LOUTH: Ollie McDonnell 0-3; Paddy Keenan 0-2; Darren Clarke 0-1; Mark Stanfield 0-1; Paddy Matthews 0-1

WEXFORD
John Cooper

Colm Morris   Philip Wallace   Niall Murphy

Darragh Breen   David Murphy   George Sunderland

Paddy Colfer   Willie Carley

David Fogarty   John Hudson   Redmond Barry

John Hegarty   Darren Foran   Matty Forde (*Captain*)

SUBSTITUTES: Nicky Lambert for Willie Carley; Pat Forde for Redmond Barry; Jason Lawlor for John Hegarty; Leigh O'Brien for Darragh Breen; Gary O'Grady for John Hudson

LOUTH
Shane McCoy

Simon Gerard   Jonathan Clerkin   Jamie Carr

Alan Page   Paudie Mallon   Ray Rooney

David Devaney   Paddy Keenan

Ray Finnegan   Darren Clarke   Ray Kelly

Ollie McDonnell (*Captain*)   David Reid   Paddy Matthews

SUBSTITUTES: Derek Shevlin for Paudie Mallon; Aaron Hoey for Darren Clarke; Mark Stanfield for David Reid; Seán O'Neill for Paddy Matthews; Cormac Malone for David Devaney

LEINSTER SENIOR FOOTBALL CHAMPIONSHIP FIRST ROUND

WESTMEATH VERSUS OFFALY
CROKE PARK
REFEREE: PADDY RUSSELL (TIPPERARY)
RESULT: WESTMEATH 0-11 OFFALY 0-10

SCORERS – WESTMEATH: Dessie Dolan 0-5; Brian Morley 0-2; Fergal Wilson 0-1; Denis Glennon 0-1; Michael Ennis 0-1; J.P. Casey 0-1

SCORERS – OFFALY: James Coughlan 0-3; Paschal Kelleghan 0-2; James Grennan 0-1; Neville Coughlan 0-1; Karol Slattery 0-1; Ciarán McManus 0-1; Thomas Deehan 0-1

WESTMEATH
Gary Connaughton

James Davitt	Donal O'Donoghue	John Keane
Michael Ennis	Damien Healy	Derek Heavin
Rory O'Connell	David O'Shaughnessy (*Captain*)	
Brian Morley	Gary Dolan	Alan Mangan
Fergal Wilson	Denis Glennon	Dessie Dolan

SUBSTITUTES: J.P. Casey for Fergal Wilson; Paul Conway for Gary Dolan; Shane Colleary for Alan Mangan; Joe Fallon for J.P. Casey

OFFALY
Padraig Kelly

Shane Sullivan	Conor Evans	Scott Brady
Barry Mooney	Cathal Daly	Karol Slattery
Ciarán McManus (*Captain*)	James Grennan	
Paschal Kelleghan	Roy Malone	Alan McNamee
Colm Quinn	Neville Coughlan	Niall McNamee

SUBSTITUTES: James Coughlan for Colm Quinn; Mark Daly for Roy Malone; Thomas Deehan for Alan McNamee; Barry Malone for Shane Sullivan; Cillian Farrell for Niall McNamee

Dessie Dolan, Westmeath

Seán Boylan, Meath Manag

Daithí Regan, Meath

LEINSTER SENIOR FOOTBALL CHAMPIONSHIP FIRST ROUND

MEATH VERSUS WICKLOW
CROKE PARK
REFEREE: JIMMY MCKEE (ARMAGH)
RESULT: MEATH 2-13   WICKLOW 1-8

SCORERS – MEATH: Daithí Regan 1-5; Donal Curtis 1-0; Evan Kelly 0-2; Trevor Giles 0-2; Charles McCarthy 0-2; Stephen MacGabhann 0-1; Shane McKeigue 0-1

SCORERS – WICKLOW: Tommy Gill 0-4; Donal McGillycuddy 1-0; Brendáin Ó hAnnaidh 0-1; Alan Ellis 0-1; Tony Hannon 0-1; Wayne O'Gorman 0-1

MEATH
David Gallagher

Niall McKeigue   Darren Fay   Mark O'Reilly

Paddy Reynolds (*Captain*)   Tomás O'Connor   Stephen MacGabhann

Nigel Crawford   Anthony Moyles

Niall Kelly   Charles McCarthy   Trevor Giles

Evan Kelly   Shane McKeigue   Daithí Regan

SUBSTITUTES: Richie Kealy for Niall McKeigue; Donal Curtis for Niall Kelly; John Cullinane for Anthony Moyles; David Crimmins for Evan Kelly; Brian Farrell for Daithí Regan

WICKLOW
Robert Hollingsworth

Ciaran Hyland   Stevie Cushe   Tom Burke

Clive Davis   Stephen Byrne   Adrian Foley

Barry Sheehan   Brendáin Ó hAnnaidh

Thomas Harney   Ronan Coffey   Alan Ellis

Tommy Gill (*Captain*)   Tony Hannon   Wayne O'Gorman

SUBSTITUTES: Ciaran Clancy for Barry Sheehan; Donal McGillycuddy for Alan Ellis; Leighton Glynn for Tony Hannon; Anthony Nolan for Thomas Harney; Dara Ó hAnnaidh for Clive Davis

LEINSTER SENIOR FOOTBALL CHAMPIONSHIP FIRST ROUND

LAOIS VERSUS CARLOW
DR CULLEN PARK (CARLOW)
REFEREE: MICHAEL RYAN (LIMERICK)
RESULT: LAOIS 0-15 CARLOW 1-7

SCORERS – LAOIS: Ross Munnelly 0-4; Brian 'Beano' McDonald 0-3;
Chris Conway 0-2; Michael Lawlor 0-2; Darren Rooney 0-1; Padraig Clancy 0-1;
Kevin Fitzpatrick 0-1; Colm Parkinson 0-1

SCORERS – CARLOW: Brian Kelly 1-3; Simon Rea 0-2; Seán Kavanagh 0-1;
Mark Carpenter 0-1

LAOIS
Fergal Byron
Aidan Fennelly   Colm Byrne   Joe Higgins
Darren Rooney   Tom Kelly   Paul McDonald
Kevin Fitzpatrick   Noel Garvan
Ross Munnelly   Ian Fitzgerald   Colm Parkinson
Brian 'Beano' McDonald   Michael Lawlor   Chris Conway (*Captain*)

SUBSTITUTES: Shane Cooke for Brian 'Beano' McDonald;
Padraig Clancy for Ian Fitzgerald; Padraig McMahon for Colm Parkinson

CARLOW
James Clarke
Paul Cashin   Brian Farrell   Cormac McCarthy
Barry English   John Hayden   Joe Byrne
Thomas Walsh   Willie Power
Seán Kavanagh   Johnny Nevin   Mark Carpenter (*Captain*)
Simon Rea   Patrick Hickey   Brian Kelly

SUBSTITUTES: Johnny Kavanagh for Barry English; Brian Carbery for Patrick Hickey;
David Byrne for Cormac McCarthy; Ray Walker for Simon Rea;
Mark Brennan for Thomas Walsh

LEINSTER SENIOR FOOTBALL CHAMPIONSHIP QUARTER-FINAL

WESTMEATH VERSUS DUBLIN
CROKE PARK
REFEREE: MICHAEL COLLINS (CORK)
RESULT: WESTMEATH 0-14 DUBLIN 0-12

SCORERS – WESTMEATH: Dessie Dolan 0-3; Paul Conway 0-2; Denis Glennon 0-2; Alan Mangan 0-2; Brian Morley 0-1; Gary Dolan 0-1; David Mitchell 0-1; Fergal Wilson 0-1; Joe Fallon 0-1

SCORERS – DUBLIN: Alan Brogan 0-4; Jason Sherlock 0-4; Senan Connell 0-2; Bryan Cullen 0-1; Colin Moran 0-1

WESTMEATH
Gary Connaughton

Michael Ennis   John Keane   James Davitt

Derek Heavin   Damien Healy   Donal O'Donoghue

Gary Dolan   David O'Shaughnessy (*Captain*)

Brian Morley   Paul Conway   Alan Mangan

Fergal Wilson   Denis Glennon   Dessie Dolan

SUBSTITUTES: David Kilmartin for James Davitt; David Mitchell for Fergal Wilson; Joe Fallon for Denis Glennon

DUBLIN
Bryan Murphy

Barry Cahill   Paddy Christie   Paul Griffin

Shane Ryan   Darren Magee   Peadar Andrews

Ciarán Whelan (*Captain*)   Darren Homan

Conal Keaney   Bryan Cullen   Colin Moran

Alan Brogan   Jason Sherlock   Senan Connell

SUBSTITUTES: Ray Cosgrove for Conal Keaney; Coman Goggins for Darren Homan; Declan Lally for Bryan Cullen; Tomás Quinn for Colin Moran

Tommy Lyons, Dublin Manager 2004

LEINSTER SENIOR FOOTBALL CHAMPIONSHIP QUARTER-FINAL

WEXFORD VERSUS KILDARE
CROKE PARK
REFEREE: MICHAEL CURLEY (GALWAY)
RESULT: WEXFORD 0-12 KILDARE 0-10

SCORERS – WEXFORD: Matty Forde 0-8; Pat Forde 0-2; Jason Lawlor 0-1;
Darragh Breen 0-1

SCORERS – KILDARE: Padraig Brennan 0-2; Morgan O'Sullivan 0-2; John Doyle 0-2;
Derek McCormack 0-1; Karl Ennis 0-1; Tadhg Fennin 0-1; Padraig Hurley 0-1

WEXFORD
John Cooper

Colm Morris   Philip Wallace   Niall Murphy

Darragh Breen   David Murphy   George Sunderland

Paddy Colfer   Willie Carley

Redmond Barry   Nicky Lambert   John Hudson

John Hegarty   Darren Foran   Matty Forde (*Captain*)

SUBSTITUTES: Pat Forde for Nicky Lambert; Jason Lawlor for John Hegarty;
Leigh O'Brien for George Sunderland; Robert Hassey for Darren Foran;
Kieran Kennedy for John Hudson

KILDARE
Enda Murphy

Brian Lacey   Robbie McCabe   Andrew McLoughlin

Eamonn O'Callaghan   Michael Foley   Karl Ennis

Killian Brennan   Dermot Earley (*Captain*)

Derek McCormack   John Doyle   Alan Barry

Padraig Brennan   Morgan O'Sullivan   Tadhg Fennin

SUBSTITUTES: Padraig Hurley for Alan Barry;
Anthony Rainbow for Eamonn O'Callaghan; Padraig Donnelly for Padraig Hurley;
Glenn Ryan for Brian Lacey; Terry Rossiter for Tadhg Fennin

Matty Forde, Wexford

Pat Roe, Wexford Manager

LEINSTER SENIOR FOOTBALL CHAMPIONSHIP SEMI-FINAL

LAOIS VERSUS MEATH
CROKE PARK
REFEREE: PAT MCENANEY (MONAGHAN)
RESULT: LAOIS 1-13 MEATH 0-9

SCORERS – LAOIS: Ross Munnelly 0-6; Colm Parkinson 1-2;
Brian 'Beano' McDonald 0-2; Padraig Clancy 0-1; Michael Lawlor 0-1;
Chris Conway 0-1

SCORERS – MEATH: Joe Sheridan 0-6; Daithí Regan 0-2; Trevor Giles 0-1

LAOIS
Fergal Byron

Aidan Fennelly   Colm Byrne   Joe Higgins

Darren Rooney   Tom Kelly   Paul McDonald

Kevin Fitzpatrick   Noel Garvan

Ross Munnelly   Brian 'Beano' McDonald   Padraig Clancy

Ian Fitzgerald   Colm Parkinson   Chris Conway (*Captain*)

SUBSTITUTE: Michael Lawlor for Kevin Fitzpatrick

MEATH
David Gallagher

Niall McKeigue   Darren Fay   Mark O'Reilly

Paddy Reynolds (*Captain*)   Tomás O'Connor   Hank Traynor

Nigel Crawford   Anthony Moyles

Seamus Kenny   Charles McCarthy   Trevor Giles

Evan Kelly   Joe Sheridan   Daithí Regan

SUBSTITUTES: Donal Curtis for Evan Kelly; Ollie Murphy for Seamus Kenny;
John Cullinane for Daithí Regan; Richie Kealy for Hank Traynor;
Graham Geraghty for Tomás O'Connor

LEINSTER SENIOR FOOTBALL CHAMPIONSHIP SEMI-FINAL

WESTMEATH VERSUS WEXFORD
CROKE PARK
REFEREE: JIMMY WHITE (DONEGAL)
RESULT: WESTMEATH 2-15 WEXFORD 1-14

SCORERS – WESTMEATH: Dessie Dolan 1-7; Shane Colleary 1-0; Denis Glennon 0-2; Alan Mangan 0-2; Brian Morley 0-2; Derek Heavin 0-1; Michael Ennis 0-1

SCORERS – WEXFORD: Matty Forde 0-8; Jason Lawlor 1-1; John Hegarty 0-2; Pat Forde 0-1; Darragh Breen 0-1; David Fogarty 0-1

WESTMEATH
Gary Connaughton

John Keane	Donal O'Donoghue	James Davitt
Michael Ennis	Damien Healy	Derek Heavin
Gary Dolan	David O'Shaughnessy (*Captain*)	
Brian Morley	Paul Conway	David Mitchell
Alan Mangan	Denis Glennon	Dessie Dolan

SUBSTITUTES: Shane Colleary for Gary Dolan; Colin Galligan for David Mitchell; Joe Fallon for Brian Morley; J.P. Casey for Denis Glennon

WEXFORD
John Cooper

Darragh Breen	Philip Wallace	Niall Murphy
Redmond Barry	David Murphy	Leigh O'Brien
Paddy Colfer	Willie Carley	
David Fogarty	John Hudson	Pat Forde
Jason Lawlor	Darren Foran	Matty Forde (*Captain*)

SUBSTITUTES: John Hegarty for Darren Foran; Darren Browne for John Hudson; Robert Hassey for Pat Forde

Gary Connaughton, Westmeath

LEINSTER SENIOR FOOTBALL CHAMPIONSHIP FINAL

WESTMEATH VERSUS LAOIS
CROKE PARK
REFEREE: PAT MCENANEY (MONAGHAN)
RESULT: WESTMEATH 0-13 LAOIS 0-13 (A DRAW)

SCORERS – WESTMEATH: Denis Glennon 0-5; Dessie Dolan 0-4; Joe Fallon 0-2; Fergal Wilson 0-2

SCORERS – LAOIS: Brian 'Beano' McDonald 0-4; Chris Conway 0-2; Ross Munnelly 0-2; Shane Cooke 0-2; Darren Rooney 0-1; Michael Lawlor 0-1; Kevin Fitzpatrick 0-1

WESTMEATH
Gary Connaughton

Damien Healy   John Keane   James Davitt

Derek Heavin   Donal O'Donoghue   Michael Ennis

Gary Dolan   David O'Shaughnessy (*Captain*)

Brian Morley   Paul Conway   Fergal Wilson

Alan Mangan   Denis Glennon   Dessie Dolan

SUBSTITUTES: Rory O'Connell for Gary Dolan; Joe Fallon for Alan Mangan; Shane Colleary for Fergal Wilson; David Mitchell for Brian Morley; David Kilmartin for James Davitt

LAOIS
Fergal Byron

Aidan Fennelly   Colm Byrne   Joe Higgins

Darren Rooney   Tom Kelly   Paul McDonald

Padraig Clancy   Noel Garvan

Ross Munnelly   Kevin Fitzpatrick   Chris Conway (*Captain*)

Ian Fitzgerald   Colm Parkinson   Brian 'Beano' McDonald

SUBSTITUTES: Michael Lawlor for Ian Fitzgerald; Shane Cooke for Colm Byrne; Gary Kavanagh for Ross Munnelly; Paul Lawlor for Michael Lawlor

LEINSTER SENIOR FOOTBALL CHAMPIONSHIP FINAL REPLAY

WESTMEATH VERSUS LAOIS
CROKE PARK
REFEREE: MICK MONAHAN (KILDARE)
RESULT: WESTMEATH 0-12 LAOIS 0-10

SCORERS – WESTMEATH: Alan Mangan 0-4; Dessie Dolan 0-3; Denis Glennon 0-2; Fergal Wilson 0-1; Brian Morley 0-1; Michael Ennis 0-1

SCORERS – LAOIS: Ross Munnelly 0-3; Kevin Fitzpatrick 0-2; Tom Kelly 0-1; Padraig Clancy 0-1; Donie Brennan 0-1; Colm Parkinson 0-1; Brian 'Beano' McDonald 0-1

WESTMEATH
Gary Connaughton

| John Keane | James Davitt | Damien Healy |

Derek Heavin   Donal O'Donoghue   Michael Ennis

Rory O'Connell   David O'Shaughnessy (*Captain*)

Brian Morley   Paul Conway   Fergal Wilson

Alan Mangan   Denis Glennon   Dessie Dolan

SUBSTITUTES: Joe Fallon for Fergal Wilson; Gary Dolan for Paul Conway; Shane Colleary for Denis Glennon

LAOIS
Fergal Byron

Aidan Fennelly   Joe Higgins   Paul McDonald

Darren Rooney   Tom Kelly   Kevin Fitzpatrick

Padraig Clancy   Noel Garvan

Ross Munnelly (*Captain*)   Michael Lawlor   Gary Kavanagh

Brian 'Beano' McDonald   Donie Brennan   Colm Parkinson

SUBSTITUTES: Ian Fitzgerald for Michael Lawlor; Donal Miller for Gary Kavanagh; Martin Delaney for Donie Brennan; Paudge Conway for Joe Higgins

Ross Munnelly, Laois

Chris Conway, Laois

Here's
to the
International
Rules
Series. Here's
to the
Irish. Here's
to the Aussies.
Here's to the
fans. Here's to
the colour of match
day. Here's to the
excitement.Here's
to never giving
up. Here's to
never giving in.
Here's to winning
the 50/50s. Here's
to giving 100%. Here's
to quick hands
and even quicker
feet.Here's to the ball
in the net and points
on the board. Here's
to belief. Here's to
the pride. Here's
to the passion.
Here's to playing
for your country.
Here's to the
ultimate Test.

ROUND ONE

Fermanagh/Tipperary
Fermanagh walkover – Tipperary withdrew

12th June, St. Tighearnach's Park:
Longford 4-15   Monaghan 1-17
                         (After extra-time)

12th June, Parnell Park:
Dublin 3-24   London 0-6

12th June, Aughrim:
Derry 1-15   Wicklow 1-10

12th June, St Conleth's Park:
Offaly 2-17   Kildare 1-16

12th June, Dr.Cullen Park:
Down 1-19   Carlow 1-13

12th June, Drogheda:
Louth 2-13   Antrim 0-14
                         (After extra-time)

12th June, Cusack Park:
Clare 1-15   Sligo 1-7

ROUND TWO

3rd July, O'Moore Park:
Longford 1-14   Waterford 1-5

3rd July, Brewster Park:
Fermanagh 0-19   Meath 2-12
                         (After extra-time)

3rd July, Páirc Esler:
Tyrone 1-15   Down 0-10

3rd July, Páirc Seán Mhic Diarmada:
Dublin 1-13   Leitrim 0-4

3rd July, Parnell Park:
Galway 2-8   Louth 0-9

3rd July, Cusack Park:
Cork 0-15   Clare 0-11

4th July, Celtic Park:
Derry 0-25   Cavan 2-9
                         (After extra-time)

ROUND THREE

10th July, Wexford Park:
Wexford 2-14   Offaly 0-15

10th July, O'Moore Park:
Dublin 1-17   Longford 0-11

July 17th, Croke Park:
Fermanagh 0-18   Cork 0-12

July 17th, Croke Park:
Tyrone 1-16   Galway 0-11

July 17th, Parnell Park:
Derry 2-16   Wexford 2-5

ROUND FOUR

24th July, Dr.Hyde Park:
Derry 0-10   Limerick 0-7

24th July, St Tighearnach's Park:
Fermanagh 1-10   Donegal 0-12
                         (After extra-time)

1st August, Croke Park:
Dublin 1-14   Roscommon 0-13

1st August, Croke Park:
Tyrone 3-15   Laois 2-4

ALL-IRELAND SENIOR FOOTBALL CHAMPIONSHIP QUALIFIER ROUND ONE

LONGFORD VERSUS MONAGHAN
ST. TIGHEARNACH'S PARK (CLONES)
REFEREE: MARTY DUFFY (SLIGO)
RESULT: LONGFORD 4-15 MONAGHAN 1-17 (AFTER EXTRA-TIME)

SCORERS – LONGFORD: Padraic Davis 0-11; Paul Barden 1-1; Trevor Smullen 1-1; Liam Keenan 1-0; Declan Barden 1-0; Martin Mulleady 0-1; Stephen Lynch 0-1

SCORERS – MONAGHAN: Damien Freeman 1-3; Kieran Tavey 0-4; Rory Woods 0-3; Thomas Freeman 0-2; Gary McQuaid 0-2; Nicholas Corrigan 0-2; Dermot Duffy 0-1

LONGFORD
Damien Sheridan

Dermot Brady   Cathal Conefrey   Shane Mulligan

Martin Mulleady   Enda Ledwith   Declan Reilly

Liam Keenan   David Hannify

John Kenny   Paul Barden (*Captain*)   Paul O'Hara

Trevor Smullen   Niall Sheridan   Padraic Davis

SUBSTITUTES: David Barden for John Kenny; Arthur O'Connor for Paul O'Hara; Stephen Lynch for Shane Mulligan; Donal Ledwith for David Hannify; Shane Carroll for Martin Mulleady; EXTRA-TIME: Donal Ledwith for Arthur O'Connor; Brendan Burke for Donal Ledwith

MONAGHAN
Glenn Murphy

Padraig McKenna   James Coyle   Edmund Lennon

Gary McQuaid   John Paul Mone   Vincent Corey

Eoin Lennon   Dermot Duffy (*Captain*)

Nicholas Corrigan   Rory Woods   Dick Clerkin

Thomas Freeman   Paul Finlay   Damien Freeman

SUBSTITUTES: Michael Slowey for Paul Finlay; Kieran Tavey for Rory Woods; Jason Hughes for Padraig McKenna; EXTRA-TIME: Raymond Ronaghan for Kieran Tavey; Rory Woods for Raymond Ronaghan; Dessie Mone for Gary McQuaid; Damien Larkin for Damien Freeman

ALL-IRELAND SENIOR FOOTBALL CHAMPIONSHIP QUALIFIER ROUND ONE

DUBLIN VERSUS LONDON
PARNELL PARK (DUBLIN)
REFEREE: BRIAN TYRELL (TIPPERARY)
RESULT: DUBLIN 3-24 LONDON 0-6

SCORERS – DUBLIN: Alan Brogan 2-4; Tomás Quinn 1-5; Senan Connell 0-7; Ray Cosgrove 0-3; Colin Moran 0-2; Darren Magee 0-1; Declan O'Mahoney 0-1; Jason Sherlock 0-1

SCORERS – LONDON: Fergus McMahon 0-3; Scott Doran 0-1; Brendan Egan 0-1; Seamus Byrnes 0-1

DUBLIN
Stephen Cluxton

Barry Cahill   Paddy Christie   Paul Griffin

Shane Ryan   Darren Magee   Peadar Andrews

Ciarán Whelan (*Captain*)   Declan O'Mahoney

Colin Moran   Tomás Quinn   Senan Connell

Alan Brogan   Jason Sherlock   Johnny McNally

SUBSTITUTES: Paul Casey for Shane Ryan; David Henry for Paul Griffin; Coman Goggins for Peadar Andrews; Declan Lally for Johnny McNally; Ray Cosgrove for Colin Moran

LONDON
Michael Lillis

Charles Harrisson   Brian McMonagle   Seán Murphy

Johnny Niblock (*Captain*)   Damien McKenna   Aidan McLarnon

Gary Kane   Paddy Quinn

Scott Doran   Fergus McMahon   Gordon Weldon

Brendan Egan   Darragh Kinneavy   Patrick Lynott

SUBSTITUTES: Paddy McGonigle for Johnny Niblock; Teu Ó hAilpín for Patrick Lynott; Carl Scanlon for Gordon Weldon; Seamus Byrnes for Aidan McLarnon

ALL-IRELAND SENIOR FOOTBALL CHAMPIONSHIP QUALIFIER
ROUND ONE

DERRY VERSUS WICKLOW
AUGHRIM (WICKLOW)
REFEREE: PADDY RUSSELL (TIPPERARY)
RESULT: DERRY 1-15 WICKLOW 1-10

SCORERS – DERRY: Paddy Bradley 1-8; Johnny McBride 0-4; James Donaghy 0-3

SCORERS – WICKLOW: Trevor Doyle 1-5; Tommy Gill 0-3; Paddy Dalton 0-1;
Ronan Coffey 0-1

DERRY
Barry Gillis

Kevin McGuckin   Niall McCusker   Gerard O'Kane

Francis McEldowney   Seán Marty Lockhart (*Captain*)   Padraig Kelly

Fergal Doherty   Patsy Bradley

James Donaghy   Johnny McBride   Conleth Moran

Jim Kelly   Paddy Bradley   Eamonn Burke

SUBSTITUTE: Conleith Gilligan for Jim Kelly

WICKLOW
Robert Hollingsworth

Ciaran Hyland   Stevie Cushe   Tom Burke

Leighton Glynn   Dara Ó hAnnaidh   Adrian Foley

Brendáin Ó hAnnaidh   Gary Doran

Thomas Harney   Trevor Doyle (*Captain*)   Alan Ellis

Tommy Gill   Ronan Coffey   Wayne O'Gorman

SUBSTITUTES: Ciaran Clancy for Dara Ó hAnnaidh; Paddy Dalton for Thomas Harney;
Paul Cronin for Wayne O'Gorman; Barry Mernagh for Adrian Foley;
Clive Davis for Brendáin Ó hAnnaidh

ALL-IRELAND SENIOR FOOTBALL CHAMPIONSHIP QUALIFIER ROUND ONE

OFFALY VERSUS KILDARE
ST. CONLETH'S PARK (NEWBRIDGE)
REFEREE: JOE MCQUILLAN (CAVAN)
RESULT: OFFALY 2–17 KILDARE 1–16

SCORERS – OFFALY: James Coughlan 0-6; Paschal Kelleghan 1-3; Niall McNamee 1-0; Neville Coughlan 0-2; Thomas Deehan 0-2; Mark Daly 0-2; James Grennan 0-1; Ciarán McManus 0-1

SCORERS – KILDARE: John Doyle 0-8; Tadhg Fennin 1-3; Michael Foley 0-1; Glenn Ryan 0-1; Dermot Earley 0-1; Padraig Donnelly 0-1; Derek McCormack 0-1

OFFALY
Padraig Kelly

Shane Sullivan   Conor Evans   Scott Brady

Barry Mooney   Cathal Daly   Karol Slattery

Mark Daly   James Grennan

Niall McNamee   Paschal Kelleghan   Ciarán McManus (*Captain*)

James Coughlan   Neville Coughlan   Thomas Deehan

SUBSTITUTES: John O'Neill for Mark Daly; Alan McNamee for James Grennan; Colm Quinn for Paschal Kelleghan; Roy Malone for Niall McNamee; John Reynolds for Thomas Deehan

KILDARE
Enda Murphy

Damien Hendy   Robbie McCabe   Andrew McLoughlin

Eamonn O'Callaghan   Michael Foley   Glenn Ryan

Dermot Earley (*Captain*)   Killian Brennan

Karl Ennis   Morgan O'Sullivan   Derek McCormack

Terry Rossiter   Padraig Donnelly   John Doyle

SUBSTITUTES: Eamonn Fitzpatrick for Damien Hendy; Tadhg Fennin for Terry Rossiter; Willie Heffernan for Killian Brennan; Alan Barry for Padraig Donnelly; Anthony Rainbow for Robbie McCabe

ALL-IRELAND SENIOR FOOTBALL CHAMPIONSHIP QUALIFIER ROUND ONE

DOWN VERSUS CARLOW
DR. CULLEN PARK (CARLOW)
REFEREE: JOHN GEANEY (CORK)
RESULT: DOWN 1-19 CARLOW 1-13

SCORERS – DOWN: Benny Coulter 1-3; Daniel Hughes 0-4; Aidan O'Prey 0-3; Liam Doyle 0-3; Shane Ward 0-2; Gregory McCartan 0-2; John Clarke 0-1; Ronan Murtagh 0-1

SCORERS – CARLOW: Simon Rea 0-7; Mark Carpenter 1-1; Brian Carbery 0-2; Brian Kelly 0-1; Willie Power 0-1; Johnny Nevin 0-1

DOWN
Mickey McVeigh

Brendan Grant	Alan Molloy	Adrian Scullion
John Clarke	Martin Cole	Seán Farrell
Dan Gordon	Gregory McCartan (*Captain*)	
Eoin McCartan	Shane Ward	Ronan Sexton
Benny Coulter	Aidan O'Prey	Daniel Hughes

SUBSTITUTES: Ronan Murtagh for Eoin McCartan; Liam Doyle for Gregory McCartan; Aidan Brannigan for Seán Farrell; Colin McCrickard for Brendan Grant; Stephen Kearney for Daniel Hughes

CARLOW
James Clarke

Paul Cashin	Brian Farrell	Cormac McCarthy
Johnny Kavanagh	John Hayden	Joe Byrne
David Byrne	Willie Power	
Seán Kavanagh	Johnny Nevin	Mark Carpenter (*Captain*)
Simon Rea	Brian Carbery	Brian Kelly

SUBSTITUTES: Mark Brennan for David Byrne; Thomas Walsh for Johnny Nevin; Stephen O'Brien for Joe Byrne; Patrick Hickey for Brian Kelly; Ken Walker for Cormac McCarthy

ALL-IRELAND SENIOR FOOTBALL CHAMPIONSHIP QUALIFIER ROUND ONE

LOUTH VERSUS ANTRIM
DROGHEDA G.A.A. GROUNDS
REFEREE: PAT MCGOVERN (GALWAY)
RESULT: LOUTH 2-13 ANTRIM 0-14 (AFTER EXTRA-TIME)

SCORERS – LOUTH: Mark Stanfield 1-2; J.P. Rooney 1-1; Aaron Hoey 0-3; Paddy Keenan 0-2; David Devaney 0-1; Nicky McDonnell 0-1; Ollie McDonnell 0-1; Darren Clarke 0-1; Derek Shevlin 0-1

SCORERS – ANTRIM: Kevin Madden 0-7; Kevin McGourty 0-3; Gearóid Adams 0-1; Kevin Brady 0-1; Andrew McClean 0-1; Seán Kelly 0-1

LOUTH
Shane McCoy
Jonathan Clerkin   Paudie Mallon   Jamie Carr
Derek Shevlin   Simon Gerard   Ray Rooney
David Devaney   Paddy Keenan
Ray Kelly   David Reid   Nicky McDonnell
Aaron Hoey   Mark Stanfield   Ollie McDonnell (*Captain*)

SUBSTITUTES: Alan Page for David Reid; Darren Clarke for Ray Kelly; J.P. Rooney for Nicky McDonnell; Paddy Matthews for Aaron Hoey

* Alan Page was sent-off in normal time –
Nicky McDonnell came on in extra-time to bring Louth back up to fifteen players.

ANTRIM
Seán McGreevy
Niall Ward   Colin Brady   Tony Convery
Gearóid Adams   Seán Kelly   Anto Finnegan
Joe Quinn   Mark McCrory
Martin McCarry   Kevin McGourty   James Marron
Kevin Brady (*Captain*)   Darren O'Hare   Kevin Madden

SUBSTITUTES: Kevin Niblock for Joe Quinn; John McKeever for Tony Convery; Andrew McClean for James Marron; Mark Dougan for Darren O'Hare; Kevin Murray for Seán Kelly

ALL-IRELAND SENIOR FOOTBALL CHAMPIONSHIP QUALIFIER ROUND ONE

CLARE VERSUS SLIGO
CUSACK PARK (ENNIS)
REFEREE: MAURICE DEEGAN (LAOIS)
RESULT: CLARE 1-15 SLIGO 1-7

SCORERS – CLARE: Denis Russell 1-5; Michael O'Dwyer 0-5; Colm Mullen 0-1; Alan Clohessy 0-1; Enda Coughlan 0-1; Ger Quinlan 0-1; Seán O'Meara 0-1

SCORERS – SLIGO: Michael McNamara 1-1; Gerry McGowan 0-3; Dessie Sloyan 0-1; Kieran Quinn 0-1; Mark Brehony 0-1

CLARE
Dermot O'Brien

Padraig Gallagher	Conor Whelan	Kevin Dilleen
Alan Clohessy	Brian Considine	Ronan Slattery
David Russell (Kilkee) (*Captain*)		Ger Quinlan
Denis Russell	Colm Mullen	Mícheál O'Shea
Enda Coughlan	Odhran O'Dwyer	Michael O'Dwyer

SUBSTITUTES: Evan Talty for Kevin Dilleen; Stephen Hickey for Mícheál O'Shea; Seán O'Meara for Colm Mullen; Ciarán Considine for Michael O'Dwyer; Dara Blake for Evan Talty

SLIGO
Philip Greene

Johnny Martyn	Noel McGuire	Neil Carew
Padraic Doohan	Nigel Clancy	Michael Langan
Kieran Quinn		Seán Davey
Eamonn O'Hara (*Captain*)	Brian Curran	Dara McGarty
Dessie Sloyan	Paul Taylor	Michael McNamara

SUBSTITUTES: Gerry McGowan for Paul Taylor; Mark Brehony for Dara McGarty; Jonathan Davey for Neil Carew; David Durkin for Nigel Clancy; Paul Durcan for Seán Davey

J.P. Rooney, Louth

Paddy Bradley, Derry

ALL-IRELAND SENIOR FOOTBALL CHAMPIONSHIP QUALIFIER ROUND TWO

LONGFORD VERSUS WATERFORD
O'MOORE PARK (PORTLAOISE)
REFEREE: JIMMY MCKEE (ARMAGH)
RESULT: LONGFORD 1–14 WATERFORD 1–5

SCORERS – LONGFORD: Padraic Davis 1-4; Paul Barden 0-4; Trevor Smullen 0-2; Niall Sheridan 0-2; David Hannify 0-1; David Barden 0-1

SCORERS – WATERFORD: Lee Hayes 1-2; Billy Harty 0-1; Connie Power 0-1; John Moore 0-1

LONGFORD
Damien Sheridan

Dermot Brady   Cathal Conefrey   Brendan Burke

Martin Mulleady   Enda Ledwith   Declan Reilly

Liam Keenan   David Hannify

Arthur O'Connor   Paul Barden (*Captain*)   Trevor Smullen

David Barden   Niall Sheridan   Padraic Davis

SUBSTITUTES: Shane Mulligan for Martin Mulleady;
Shane Carroll for Arthur O'Connor; Brian Sheridan for Dermot Brady;
Jamesie Martin for Niall Sheridan; Enda Williams for Padraic Davis

WATERFORD
Paul Hoolihan

Kieran Connery   Karl O'Keeffe   Trevor Costelloe

Edmund Rockett   Andy Hubbard   Niall Hennessy

William Kavanagh   Paul Ogle

Liam Ó Lionáin   Peter Queally   Ger Power (*Captain*)

Billy Harty   John Hearne   Niall Curran

SUBSTITUTES: Lee Hayes for Liam Ó Lionáin; Connie Power for Peter Queally;
Tomás Dunphy for William Kavanagh; Tony Whelan for Paul Ogle;
John Moore for Billy Harty

ALL-IRELAND SENIOR FOOTBALL CHAMPIONSHIP QUALIFIER ROUND TWO

FERMANAGH VERSUS MEATH
BREWSTER PARK (ENNISKILLEN)
REFEREE: MICHAEL DALY (MAYO)
RESULT: FERMANAGH 0-19 MEATH 2-12 (AFTER EXTRA-TIME)

SCORERS – FERMANAGH: Colm Bradley 0-6; Stephen Maguire 0-3; Mark Little 0-3; James Sherry 0-2; Eamonn Maguire 0-2; Ciarán O'Reilly 0-2; Darragh McGrath 0-1

SCORERS – MEATH: Daithí Regan 2-6; Evan Kelly 0-1; Seamus Kenny 0-1; Trevor Giles 0-1; Ollie Murphy 0-1; David Crimmins 0-1; Niall Kelly 0-1

FERMANAGH
Niall Tinney

Niall Bogue   Barry Owens   Hughie Brady

Raymond Johnston   Shane McDermott (*Captain*)   Declan O'Reilly

Marty McGrath   Liam McBarron

Eamonn Maguire   James Sherry   Mark Little

Ciarán O'Reilly   Stephen Maguire   Colm Bradley

SUBSTITUTES: Ryan McCluskey for Liam McBarron; Peter Sherry for Barry Owens; Shane Goan for Declan O'Reilly; Darragh McGrath for Stephen Maguire; Extra-time: Ciarán Boyle for Hughie Brady; Eamonn Sherry for Ciarán O'Reilly

MEATH
David Gallagher

Niall McKeigue   Darren Fay   Mark O'Reilly

Paddy Reynolds (*Captain*) Tomás O'Connor   Trevor Giles

Nigel Crawford   Anthony Moyles

Evan Kelly   Charles McCarthy   Seamus Kenny

Daithí Regan   Shane McKeigue   Joe Sheridan

SUBSTITUTES: Ollie Murphy for Charles McCarthy; David Crimmins for Shane McKeigue; Niall Kelly for Tomás O'Connor; Damien Byrne for Niall Kelly; Extra-time: Donal Curtis for Daithí Regan; Charles McCarthy for Damien Byrne

ALL-IRELAND SENIOR FOOTBALL CHAMPIONSHIP QUALIFIER ROUND TWO

TYRONE VERSUS DOWN
PÁIRC ESLER (NEWRY)
REFEREE: MICHAEL MONAHAN (KILDARE)
RESULT: TYRONE 1-15 DOWN 0-10

SCORERS – TYRONE: Mark Harte 0-7; Seán Cavanagh 1-1; Owen Mulligan 0-3; Brian McGuigan 0-2; Colm McCullagh 0-2

SCORERS – DOWN: Liam Doyle 0-3; John Clarke 0-2; Martin Cole 0-1; Gregory McCartan 0-1; Benny Coulter 0-1; Aidan O'Prey 0-1; Colin McCrickard 0-1

TYRONE
Pascal McConnell
Ryan McMenamin   Conor Gormley   Ciarán Gourley
Joe McMahon   Shane Sweeney   Philip Jordan
Kevin Hughes   Seán Cavanagh
Brian Dooher (*Captain*)   Brian McGuigan   Ger Cavlan
Mark Harte   Owen Mulligan   Stephen O'Neill

SUBSTITUTE: Colm McCullagh for Stephen O'Neill

DOWN
Mickey McVeigh
Michael Higgins   Alan Molloy   Adrian Scullion
John Clarke   Martin Cole   Seán Farrell
Dan Gordon   Gregory McCartan (*Captain*)
Liam Doyle   Shane Ward   Ronan Murtagh
Benny Coulter   Aidan O'Prey   Daniel Hughes

SUBSTITUTES: Brendan Grant for Adrian Scullion; Seán Ward for Gregory McCartan; Colin McCrickard for Shane Ward; Eoin McCartan for Aidan O'Prey; Aidan Fagan for Ronan Murtagh

RESPECT

PROUD SPONSORS OF THE GAA All Stars

vodafone™

ALL-IRELAND SENIOR FOOTBALL CHAMPIONSHIP QUALIFIER ROUND TWO

DUBLIN VERSUS LEITRIM
PÁIRC SEÁN MHIC DIARMADA (CARRICK-ON-SHANNON)
REFEREE: BRIAN CROWE (CAVAN)
RESULT: DUBLIN 1-13 LEITRIM 0-4

SCORERS – DUBLIN: Senan Connell 1-2; Tomás Quinn 0-3; Alan Brogan 0-3; Jason Sherlock 0-2; Paul Casey 0-1; Bryan Cullen 0-1; Dessie Farrell 0-1

SCORERS – LEITRIM: Michael Foley 0-2; Barry Prior 0-1; Fintan McBrien 0-1

DUBLIN
Stephen Cluxton

Barry Cahill   Paddy Christie   Coman Goggins

Paul Casey   Bryan Cullen   Paul Griffin

Jonathan Magee   Darren Magee

Senan Connell   Ciarán Whelan (*Captain*)   Declan Lally

Alan Brogan   Jason Sherlock   Tomás Quinn

SUBSTITUTES: Ian Robertson for Declan Lally; Dessie Farrell for Tomás Quinn; Ray Cosgrove for Jason Sherlock; Declan O'Mahoney for Darren Magee; Shane Ryan for Jonathan Magee

LEITRIM
Gareth Phelan

Dermot Reynolds   Seamus Quinn   Michael McGuinness

Niall Gilbane   Padraig Flynn   Colin Regan

Noel Doonan   Chris Carroll (*Captain*)

James Glancy   Jimmy Guckian   Barry Prior

John McGuinness   Pat Farrell   Michael Foley

SUBSTITUTES: Fintan McBrien for John McGuinness; Shane Canning for Pat Farrell; Philly McGuinness for James Glancy; Declan Gilhooley for Michael Foley

ALL-IRELAND SENIOR FOOTBALL CHAMPIONSHIP QUALIFIER ROUND TWO

GALWAY VERSUS LOUTH
PARNELL PARK (DUBLIN)
REFEREE: JOE MCQUILLAN (CAVAN)
RESULT: GALWAY 2-8 LOUTH 0-9

SCORERS - GALWAY: Padraic Joyce 1-3; Noel Meehan 1-0; Michael Donnellan 0-2; Kevin Walsh 0-1; Derek Savage 0-1; Matthew Clancy 0-1

SCORERS - LOUTH: Mark Stanfield 0-5; J.P Rooney 0-2; Nicky McDonnell 0-1; Paddy Keenan 0-1

GALWAY
Brian O'Donoghue

Kieran Fitzgerald   Gary Fahey   Tomás Meehan

Declan Meehan (*Captain*)   Paul Clancy   Barry Dooney

Michael Donnellan   Kevin Walsh

Joe Bergin   Padraic Joyce   Matthew Clancy

Derek Savage   Michael Meehan   Tommie Joyce

SUBSTITUTES: Noel Meehan for Tommie Joyce; Damien Burke for Barry Dooney; John Devane for Matthew Clancy

LOUTH
Shane McCoy

Alan Page   Paudie Mallon   Jamie Carr

Derek Shevlin   Simon Gerard   Ray Rooney

David Devaney   Paddy Keenan

Ray Finnegan   Ollie McDonnell (*Captain*)   Nicky McDonnell

Aaron Hoey   Mark Stanfield   J.P. Rooney

SUBSTITUTES: Darren Clarke for Ollie McDonnell; Paddy Matthews for David Devaney; Ray Kelly for Mark Stanfield

ALL-IRELAND SENIOR FOOTBALL CHAMPIONSHIP QUALIFIER ROUND TWO

CORK VERSUS CLARE
CUSACK PARK (ENNIS)
REFEREE: SEAMUS MCCORMACK (MEATH)
RESULT: CORK 0-15 CLARE 0-11

SCORERS – CORK: Colin Corkery 0-6; Colin Crowley 0-2;
Brendan Jer O'Sullivan 0-1; Micheál Ó Croinín 0-1; Alan Cronin 0-1;
Ciarán O'Sullivan 0-1; Micheál O'Sullivan 0-1; Conor McCarthy 0-1; Eoin Sexton 0-1

SCORERS – CLARE: Denis Russell 0-7; Alan Clohessy 0-2; Rory Donnelly 0-1;
David Russell (Kilkee) 0-1

CORK
Kevin O'Dwyer
Seán O'Brien   Derek Kavanagh   Gary Murphy
Eoin Sexton   Graham Canty   Martin Cronin
Dermot Hurley   Nicholas Murphy
Alan Cronin   Micheál Ó Croinín   Conor McCarthy
Colin Crowley (*Captain*)   Colin Corkery   Brendan Jer O'Sullivan

SUBSTITUTES: Ciarán O'Sullivan for Brendan Jer O'Sullivan;
Micheál O'Sullivan for Dermot Hurley; Seán Levis for Micheál Ó Croinín;
Kevin O'Sullivan for Alan Cronin

CLARE
Dermot O'Brien
Padraig Gallagher   Conor Whelan   Kevin Dilleen
Alan Clohessy   Brian Considine   Ronan Slattery
David Russell (Kilkee) (*Captain*)   Ger Quinlan
Denis Russell   Stephen Hickey   Odhran O'Dwyer
Enda Coughlan   Micheál O'Shea   Rory Donnelly

SUBSTITUTES: Noel Griffin for Brian Considine; Seán O'Meara for Odhran O'Dwyer;
Donal O'Sullivan for Stephen Hickey; David Russell (Clarecastle) for Micheál O'Shea

ALL-IRELAND SENIOR FOOTBALL CHAMPIONSHIP QUALIFIER ROUND TWO

DERRY VERSUS CAVAN
CELTIC PARK (DERRY)
REFEREE: JOHN BANNON (LONGFORD)
RESULT: DERRY 0-25 CAVAN 2-9 (AFTER EXTRA-TIME)

SCORERS – DERRY: Paddy Bradley 0-8; Enda Muldoon 0-7; Johnny McBride 0-2; James Donaghy 0-1; Niall McCusker 0-1; Padraig Kelly 0-1; Fergal Doherty 0-1; Patsy Bradley 0-1; Paul McFlynn 0-1; Conleith Gilligan 0-1; Conleth Moran 0-1

SCORERS – CAVAN: Gerald Pierson 1-1; Micheál Lyng 0-4; Jason O'Reilly 1-0; Mark McKeever 0-3; Larry Reilly 0-1

DERRY
Barry Gillis

Kevin McGuckin   Niall McCusker   Gerard O'Kane

Francis McEldowney   Padraig O'Kane   Padraig Kelly

Fergal Doherty   Patsy Bradley

James Donaghy   Johnny McBride   Conleth Moran

Johnny Bradley   Paddy Bradley (*Captain*)   Enda Muldoon

SUBSTITUTES: Paul McFlynn for Padraig O'Kane; Conleith Gilligan for Conleth Moran; Fergal McEldowney for James Donaghy

CAVAN
Eoghan Elliott

Cathal Collins   Darren Rabbitte   Anthony Forde

Eamonn Reilly   Anthony Gaynor   Karl Crotty

Trevor Crowe   Shane Cole

Michael Brides   Mícheál Lyng   Mark McKeever

Larry Reilly (*Captain*)   Gerald Pierson   Jason O'Reilly

SUBSTITUTES: Dermot McCabe for Michael Brides; Rory Donohoe for Cathal Collins; Michael Hannon for Karl Crotty; EXTRA-TIME: Paul Brady for Eamonn Reilly; Nicholas Walsh for Shane Cole; Seánie Johnston for Gerald Pierson

ALL-IRELAND SENIOR FOOTBALL CHAMPIONSHIP QUALIFIER ROUND THREE

WEXFORD VERSUS OFFALY
WEXFORD PARK (WEXFORD)
REFEREE: AIDAN MANGAN (KERRY)
RESULT: WEXFORD 2-14 OFFALY 0-15

SCORERS – WEXFORD: Matty Forde 2-10; Redmond Barry 0-1; Willie Carley 0-1; Jason Lawlor 0-1; David Fogarty 0-1

SCORERS – OFFALY: James Coughlan 0-7; Colm Quinn 0-2; Mark Daly 0-1; Paschal Kelleghan 0-1; James Grennan 0-1; Neville Coughlan 0-1; John Reynolds 0-1; Shane Sullivan 0-1

WEXFORD
John Cooper

Colm Morris   Philip Wallace   Niall Murphy

Darragh Breen   David Murphy   Leigh O'Brien

Paddy Colfer   Willie Carley

Redmond Barry   Pat Forde   David Fogarty

Jason Lawlor   Darren Browne   Matty Forde (*Captain*)

SUBSTITUTES: John Hudson for Pat Forde; Darren Foran for Darren Browne; Robert Hassey for Willie Carley; Paraic Curtis for Leigh O'Brien

OFFALY
Padraig Kelly

Cathal Daly   Conor Evans   Scott Brady

Barry Mooney   Shane Sullivan   Karol Slattery

Mark Daly   James Grennan

Niall McNamee   Paschal Kelleghan   Ciarán McManus (*Captain*)

James Coughlan   Neville Coughlan   John Reynolds

SUBSTITUTES: Barry Malone for Cathal Daly; Roy Malone for John Reynolds; Colm Quinn for Mark Daly

ALL-IRELAND SENIOR FOOTBALL CHAMPIONSHIP QUALIFIER ROUND THREE

DUBLIN VERSUS LONGFORD
O'MOORE PARK (PORTLAOISE)
REFEREE: MICHAEL CURLEY (GALWAY)
RESULT: DUBLIN 1–17 LONGFORD 0–11

SCORERS – DUBLIN: Tomás Quinn 0-5; Alan Brogan 0-4; Ian Robertson 1-1; Ciarán Whelan 0-3; Jason Sherlock 0-2; Shane Ryan 0-1; Dessie Farrell 0-1

SCORERS – LONGFORD: Padraic Davis 0-7; Trevor Smullen 0-2; David Barden 0-2

DUBLIN
Stephen Cluxton
Barry Cahill   Paddy Christie   Coman Goggins
Paul Casey   Bryan Cullen   Paul Griffin
Darren Homan   Darren Magee
Jason Sherlock   Ciarán Whelan (*Captain*)   Senan Connell
Alan Brogan   Ian Robertson   Tomás Quinn

SUBSTITUTES: Shane Ryan for Paul Casey; Dessie Farrell for Alan Brogan; Jonathan Magee for Darren Homan; Robbie Boyle for Ian Robertson; Ray Cosgrove for Senan Connell

LONGFORD
Damien Sheridan
Dermot Brady   Cathal Conefrey   Brendan Burke
Martin Mulleady   Enda Ledwith   Declan Reilly
Liam Keenan   David Hannify
Arthur O'Connor   Paul Barden (*Captain*)   Trevor Smullen
David Barden   Niall Sheridan   Padraic Davis

SUBSTITUTES: Shane Carroll for Martin Mulleady; Shane Mulligan for Shane Carroll; John Kenny for Arthur O'Connor; Paul O'Hara for Trevor Smullen

ALL-IRELAND SENIOR FOOTBALL CHAMPIONSHIP QUALIFIER ROUND THREE

FERMANAGH VERSUS CORK
CROKE PARK
REFEREE: MAURICE DEEGAN (LAOIS)
RESULT: FERMANAGH 0-18 CORK 0-12

SCORERS – FERMANAGH: Stephen Maguire 0-6; James Sherry 0-4; Mark Little 0-2; Eamonn Maguire 0-2; Tom Brewster 0-1; Marty McGrath 0-1; Colm Bradley 0-1; Declan O'Reilly 0-1

SCORERS – CORK: Colin Corkery 0-5; Brendan Jer O'Sullivan 0-2; Conor McCarthy 0-2; Graham Canty 0-1; Nicholas Murphy 0-1; Anthony Lynch 0-1

FERMANAGH
Niall Tinney

Niall Bogue   Barry Owens   Ryan McCluskey

Raymond Johnston   Shane McDermott (*Captain*)   Declan O'Reilly

Marty McGrath   Liam McBarron

Eamonn Maguire   James Sherry   Mark Little

Ciarán O'Reilly   Stephen Maguire   Colm Bradley

SUBSTITUTES: Tom Brewster for Ciarán O'Reilly; Peter Sherry for Liam McBarron; Damien Kelly for Declan O'Reilly

CORK
Kevin O'Dwyer

Seán O'Brien   Derek Kavanagh   Gary Murphy

Eoin Sexton   Seán Levis   Martin Cronin

Micheál O'Sullivan   Graham Canty

Nicholas Murphy   Ciarán O'Sullivan   Conor McCarthy

Colin Crowley (*Captain*)   Colin Corkery   Alan Cronin

SUBSTITUTES: Anthony Lynch for Seán O'Brien; Brendan Jer O'Sullivan for Seán Levis; Fionán Murray for Ciarán O'Sullivan; Kieran O'Connor for Eoin Sexton; Micheál Ó Croinín for Colin Crowley

ALL-IRELAND SENIOR FOOTBALL CHAMPIONSHIP QUALIFIER ROUND THREE

TYRONE VERSUS GALWAY
CROKE PARK
REFEREE: MICHAEL MONAHAN (KILDARE)
RESULT: TYRONE 1-16 GALWAY 0-11

SCORERS – TYRONE: Owen Mulligan 0-5; Stephen O'Neill 0-4; Seán Cavanagh 0-3; Brian McGuigan 1-0; Brian Dooher 0-1; Shane Sweeney 0-1; Philip Jordan 0-1; Peter Canavan 0-1

SCORERS – GALWAY: Padraic Joyce 0-4; Michael Donnellan 0-2; Derek Savage 0-1; Tommie Joyce 0-1; Seán Ó Domhnaill 0-1; John Devane 0-1; Tomás Meehan 0-1

TYRONE
Pascal McConnell

Ryan McMenamin   Conor Gormley   Ciarán Gourley

Joe McMahon   Shane Sweeney   Philip Jordan

Kevin Hughes   Seán Cavanagh

Brian Dooher (*Captain*)   Brian McGuigan   Ger Cavlan

Michael Coleman   Owen Mulligan   Stephen O'Neill

SUBSTITUTES: Peter Canavan for Michael Coleman; Leo Meenan for Owen Mulligan; Barry Collins for Brian Dooher

GALWAY
Brian O'Donoghue

Kieran Fitzgerald   Gary Fahey   Tomás Meehan

Damien Burke   Paul Clancy   Declan Meehan (*Captain*)

Joe Bergin   Seán Ó Domhnaill

Michael Meehan   Michael Donnellan   Matthew Clancy

Derek Savage   Padraic Joyce   John Devane

SUBSTITUTES: Tommie Joyce for Matthew Clancy; Noel Meehan for Michael Meehan; Nickey Joyce for Derek Savage; Darren Mullahy for Joe Bergin

ALL-IRELAND SENIOR FOOTBALL CHAMPIONSHIP QUALIFIER ROUND THREE

DERRY VERSUS WEXFORD
PARNELL PARK (DUBLIN)
REFEREE: JOHN GEANEY (CORK)
RESULT: DERRY 2-16 WEXFORD 2-5

SCORERS – DERRY: Paddy Bradley 0-8; Enda Muldoon 1-5; Dominic McIlvar 1-0; James Donaghy 0-1; Conleith Gilligan 0-1; Johnny McBride 0-1

SCORERS – WEXFORD: Matty Forde 1-4; Paddy Colfer 1-0; John Hudson 0-1

DERRY
Barry Gillis

Kevin McGuckin   Niall McCusker   Gerard O'Kane

Francis McEldowney   Paul McFlynn   Padraig Kelly

Fergal Doherty   Patsy Bradley

James Donaghy   Johnny McBride   Conleth Moran

Johnny Bradley   Paddy Bradley (*Captain*)   Enda Muldoon

SUBSTITUTES: Seán Marty Lockhart for Padraig Kelly; Conleith Gilligan for James Donaghy; Dominic McIlvar for Johnny Bradley; Eamonn Burke for Enda Muldoon; Padraig O'Kane for Kevin McGuckin

WEXFORD
John Cooper

Paraic Curtis   Philip Wallace   Niall Murphy

Darragh Breen   David Murphy   Leigh O'Brien

Paddy Colfer   Willie Carley

John Hudson   Pat Forde   David Fogarty

Jason Lawlor   Redmond Barry   Matty Forde (*Captain*)

SUBSTITUTES: Jim Darcy for Pat Forde; Kieran Kennedy for John Hudson; Diarmuid Kinsella for Willie Carley; George Sunderland for Leigh O'Brien; John Hegarty for Jason Lawlor

ALL-IRELAND SENIOR FOOTBALL CHAMPIONSHIP QUALIFIER ROUND FOUR

DERRY VERSUS LIMERICK
DR HYDE PARK (ROSCOMMON)
REFEREE: DAVID COLDRICK (MEATH)
RESULT: DERRY 0-10 LIMERICK 0-7

SCORERS – DERRY: Enda Muldoon 0-4; Paddy Bradley 0-2; Conleth Moran 0-2; Gavin Donaghy 0-1; Johnny McBride 0-1

SCORERS – LIMERICK: Eoin Keating 0-3; Conor Fitzgerald 0-2; Muiris Gavin 0-1; Mike O'Brien 0-1

DERRY
Barry Gillis

Kevin McGuckin   Niall McCusker   Gerard O'Kane

Francis McEldowney   Paul McFlynn   Padraig Kelly

Fergal Doherty   Patsy Bradley

James Donaghy   Johnny McBride   Conleth Moran

Johnny Bradley   Paddy Bradley (*Captain*)   Enda Muldoon

SUBSTITUTES: Conleith Gilligan for James Donaghy; Seán Marty Lockhart for Niall McCusker; Gavin Donaghy for Conleith Gilligan; Mark Lynch for Johnny Bradley

LIMERICK
Seamus O'Donnell

Mark O'Riordan   Johnny McCarthy   Tommy Stack (*Captain*)

Conor Mullane   Stephen Lucey   Stephen Lavin

Jason Stokes   John Galvin

Stephen Kelly   Muiris Gavin   Mike O'Brien

Conor Fitzgerald   Eoin Keating   Micheál Reidy

SUBSTITUTES: John Quane for Micheál Reidy; Johnny Murphy for Muiris Gavin; Damien Reidy for Conor Mullane; Padraig Browne for Jason Stokes

ALL-IRELAND SENIOR FOOTBALL CHAMPIONSHIP QUALIFIER
ROUND FOUR
FERMANAGH VERSUS DONEGAL
ST. TIGHEARNACH'S PARK (CLONES)
REFEREE: JOE MCQUILLAN (CAVAN)
RESULT: FERMANAGH 1-10 DONEGAL 0-12 (AFTER EXTRA-TIME)

SCORERS – FERMANAGH: Stephen Maguire 0-4; Eamonn Maguire 1-0; Marty McGrath 0-2; Colm Bradley 0-2; Tom Brewster 0-1; Shane McDermott 0-1

SCORERS – DONEGAL: Brendan Devenney 0-3; Adrian Sweeney 0-2; Michael Hegarty 0-2; Brian Roper 0-2; John Gildea 0-1; Christy Toye 0-1; Colm McFadden 0-1

FERMANAGH
Niall Tinney
Niall Bogue   Barry Owens   Ryan McCluskey
Raymond Johnston Shane McDermott (*Captain*) Declan O'Reilly
Marty McGrath Liam McBarron
Eamonn Maguire Stephen Maguire   Mark Little
Ciarán O'Reilly   James Sherry   Colm Bradley

SUBSTITUTES: Damien Kelly for Declan O'Reilly; Peter Sherry for Niall Bogue; Tom Brewster for Ciarán O'Reilly; Hughie Brady for Liam McBarron; Shane Goan for Ryan McCluskey; EXTRA-TIME: Mark Murphy for James Sherry; Ryan McCluskey for Tom Brewster; Darragh McGrath for Stephen Maguire

DONEGAL
Paul Durcan
Niall McCready   Raymond Sweeney   Noel McGinley
Karl Lacey   Barry Monaghan   Shane Carr
John Gildea   Brendan Boyle
Paul McGonigle   Michael Hegarty   Brian Roper
Colm McFadden   Adrian Sweeney (*Captain*) Brendan Devenney

SUBSTITUTES: Christy Toye for Colm McFadden; Stephen McDermott for Paul McGonigle; Barry Dunnion for Noel McGinley; Stephen Cassidy for Christy Toye; EXTRA-TIME: Rory Kavanagh for Brendan Devenney, who was sent off in normal time; Colm McFadden for Stephen Cassidy; Kevin Cassidy for John Gildea; John Haran for Brian Roper; Stephen Cassidy for Adrian Sweeney

ALL-IRELAND SENIOR FOOTBALL CHAMPIONSHIP QUALIFIER ROUND FOUR

DUBLIN VERSUS ROSCOMMON
CROKE PARK
REFEREE: JOHN GEANEY (CORK)
RESULT: DUBLIN 1-14 ROSCOMMON 0-13

SCORERS – DUBLIN: Jason Sherlock 1-4; Alan Brogan 0-3; Bryan Cullen 0-2; Ciarán Whelan 0-2; Senan Connell 0-1; Conal Keaney 0-1; Darren Homan 0-1

SCORERS – ROSCOMMON: Ger Heneghan 0-5; Stephen Lohan 0-3; Nigel Dineen 0-2; Seamus O'Neill 0-1; Gary Cox 0-1; John Tiernan 0-1

DUBLIN
Stephen Cluxton

Barry Cahill   Paddy Christie   Coman Goggins

Paul Casey   Bryan Cullen   Paul Griffin

Darren Homan   Darren Magee

Conal Keaney   Ciarán Whelan (*Captain*)   Senan Connell

Alan Brogan   Ian Robertson   Jason Sherlock

SUBSTITUTES: Jonathan Magee for Darren Homan; Shane Ryan for Coman Goggins; Dessie Farrell for Conal Keaney; Tomás Quinn for Dessie Farrell

ROSCOMMON
Shane Curran (*Captain*)

Ray Cox   Michael Ryan   John Whyte

Andy McPadden   David Casey   Eamonn Towey

Seamus O'Neill   Stephen Lohan

John Hanly   Francie Grehan   Gary Cox

Jonathan Dunning   Nigel Dineen   Ger Heneghan

SUBSTITUTES: John Tiernan for Ray Cox; Karol Mannion for Stephen Lohan; Frankie Dolan for Jonathan Dunning; John Rogers for Eamonn Towey; Brian Higgins for John Hanly

ALL-IRELAND SENIOR FOOTBALL CHAMPIONSHIP QUALIFIER ROUND FOUR

TYRONE VERSUS LAOIS
CROKE PARK
REFEREE: MICHAEL COLLINS (CORK)
RESULT: TYRONE 3-15 LAOIS 2-4

SCORERS – TYRONE: Mark Harte 2-3; Owen Mulligan 1-3; Stephen O'Neill 0-3; Seán Cavanagh 0-3; Brian McGuigan 0-2; Brian Dooher 0-1

SCORERS – LAOIS: Brian 'Beano' McDonald 1-1; Kevin Fitzpatrick 1-0; Shane Cooke 0-2; Donal Miller 0-1

TYRONE
Pascal McConnell

Ryan McMenamin   Conor Gormley   Michael McGee

Joe McMahon   Shane Sweeney   Philip Jordan

Kevin Hughes   Seán Cavanagh

Brian Dooher (*Captain*)   Brian McGuigan   Ger Cavlan

Mark Harte   Owen Mulligan   Stephen O'Neill

SUBSTITUTES: Ciarán Gourley for Joe McMahon; Barry Collins for Owen Mulligan; John Devine for Pascal McConnell; Dermot Carlin for Ryan McMenamin; Chris Lawn for Shane Sweeney

LAOIS
Fergal Byron

Aidan Fennelly   Cathal Ryan   Paul McDonald

Darren Rooney   Tom Kelly   Padraig McMahon

Pauric Clancy   Noel Garvan

Ross Munnelly (*Captain*)   Kevin Fitzpatrick   Colm Parkinson

Paul Lawlor   Shane Cooke   Brian 'Beano' McDonald

SUBSTITUTES: Gary Kavanagh for Ross Munnelly; Donal Miller for Paul Lawlor; Chris Bergin for Brian 'Beano' McDonald; Paudge Conway for Cathal Ryan

Mark Harte, Tyrone

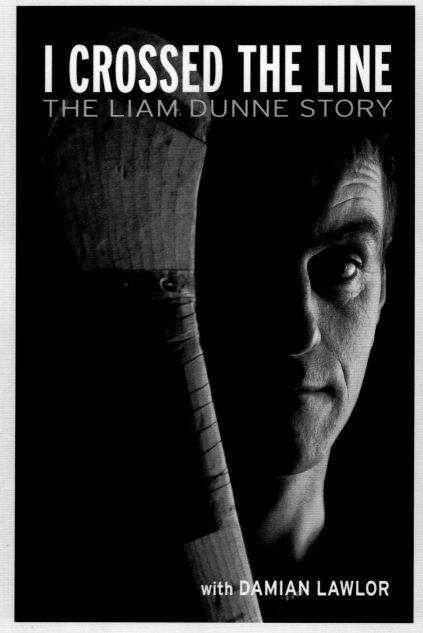

I CROSSED THE LINE
THE LIAM DUNNE STORY

with **DAMIAN LAWLOR**

Liam Dunne's best-selling autobiography
Out now in hardback and paperback

PUBLISHED BY SLIABH BÁN PRODUCTIONS

BEFORE THEY ARE FAMOUS

Hand picked while young.
Nurtured with care.
Thrown into a boiling cauldron.

Now watch them rise to the top.

Proud sponsors of The Erin Under 21 Hurling Championships

Team captain Joanne Ryan lifts the O'Duffy Cup following Tipperary's victory over Cork in the Foras na Gaeilge Senior Camogie Championship All-Ireland Final in Croke Park.

2,500 children form the letter C and the figure 100 in Páirc an Chrócaigh, before the Foras na Gaeilge All-Ireland Senior Camogie Championship Final

Tipperary fans celebrate another All-Ireland final victory

Gemma Fay, Dublin and Lisa Cohill, Galway in action in the Ladies All-Ireland Senior Football Final

Ann-Marie McDonagh, Galway and Aisling McCormack, Dublin.
TG4 Ladies All-Ireland Senior Football Final

Henry Shefflin, Kilkenny

It was a day of extra special signficance for Cork who moved back to the top on their own in the All-Ireland Roll of Honour with a sparkling second-half display of fast, attacking hurling that Kilkenny simply could not match. It was evident from the third quarter onwards that Donal O'Grady's supremely skilful Cork team would make amends for last year's defeat by the same opposition in the All-Ireland decider and that the inspirational Niall McCarthy would banish the painful memories of those missed chances twelve months previously.

In the 2003 Final, Cork outscored Kilkenny by 1-6 to a single point in the third quarter to move 1-9 to 0-11 ahead but the Munster men failed to hammer home their advantage. McCarthy was unlucky when his attempted point effort came off the upright and later on the Carrigtwohill clubman shot wide.

But what a difference a year makes! McCarthy, who had a difficult opening period against Peter Barry, was a revelation in the second half and scored three points from play – his third from long range in the 54th minute proved crucial, as it edged Cork two points clear for the first time in the match.

Ben O'Connor then stretched Cork's lead with a pointed free before another of Cork's heroes, goalkeeper Donal Óg Cusack, saved brilliantly to deny Henry Shefflin a goal that could well have changed the course of the game. Inspired by Cusack's brilliance, Cork drove on relentlessly from there to the finish and added five points without reply, including an awe-inspiring final score from Brian Corcoran, who was highly influential throughout the game and got the better of Kilkenny full-back, Noel Hickey.

Crucially, it was Corcoran, twice 'Hurler of the Year' as a defender in the nineties who landed Cork's opening score from play in the 32nd minute, which followed a largely ineffective team display during which their four points tally up to then came from three frees by the impressive Joe Deane and one from team captain Ben O'Connor. Deane also hit the crossbar with a powerful shot in the 14th minute and the Killeagh star was narrowly off target with another goal attempt in injury-time. Cork, playing against the breeze in difficult conditions, struggled in the first half hour and but for some strong defending by their under pressure backs and several missed chances by Kilkenny, the Munster men would have been considerably more than one point in arrears at half-time.

Kilkenny were clearly the better side in the opening half and almost got the dream start when Eddie Brennan had a glorious chance of a goal but shot wide after just ten seconds.

Nevertheless, Kilkenny had moved 0-6 to 0-3 ahead by the 22nd minute – with five of those points coming from play, including two from Martin Comerford and one each from James 'Cha' Fitzpatrick, Derek Lyng and Henry Shefflin, who also converted a free in the 15th minute.

Shefflin also found the target from a placed ball just before half time but Cork replied with a point from play by midfielder Jerry O'Connor.

Kilkenny paid a heavy price for missed scoring opportunities and had just a one-point advantage at the break, 0-7 to 0-6. Even though the defending champions were performing below maximum level, there were many positive aspects about their play, most notably the magnificence in defence of J.J. Delaney. Tommy Walsh was very effective; Derek Lyng was in impressive form at midfield while Shefflin, Comerford and the hard-working D.J. Carey were threatening at times. But it was evident at the interval that Kilkenny would struggle unless several of their players raised their standards considerably.

Cork had the star performer in the opening half in Fijian-born, Seán Óg Ó hAilpín, who produced an outstanding display when the need was greatest for his side and kept up the high standard for the entire game. His younger brother Setanta, who played in the 2003 final, and was later honoured with an All-Star award before signing a professional contract with Australian Rules side, Carlton, watched the game from Hill 16.

Incredibly, Kilkenny failed to score from play in the second half – a '65 and a free, both from Shefflin was the sum total of Brian Cody's side's scoring exploits. Kilkenny were held scoreless for the final twenty-five minutes and their three-in-a-row dream was well and truly dashed long before the final whistle. Cork were truly awesome after the break and swept Kilkenny aside with sheer power and pace.

Midfielders Tom Kenny and Jerry O'Connor epitomised Cork's unyielding spirit through sheer hard work and persistence. Clearly, Donal O'Grady, a modest, decent man, who avoids seeking personal plaudits, deserves tremendous credit for instilling a strong work ethic among his players. Undeniably, those who wore the Cork jersey during the year were prepared to give their all in pursuit of victory.

Niall McCarthy hit over the opening point of the second half to signal his intentions and went on to produce a storming display. Henry Shefflin sent over a '65 but the pacey Kieran Murphy replied with a finely taken point from play to level the match for the fourth time. Shefflin converted a free in the 47th minute for what amazingly transpired to be Kilkenny's last score of the match. Cork then went on the rampage and scored nine points without reply including two each from Niall McCarthy, Joe Deane and Ben O'Connor while Kieran Murphy, Tom Kenny and Brian Corcoran rowed in with a point each.

Ó hAilpín's colleagues in the half back line; Ronan Curran and John Gardiner were also impressive while behind them Diarmuid O'Sullivan was superb at full back. Wayne Sherlock and Brian Murphy, before he retired injured in the first half and John Browne when introduced from the substitutes bench, all played a huge role in Cork's victory.

Kilkenny looked weary in the third quarter and were unable to break Cork's stranglehold once the Munster side took control with their running game. Timmy McCarthy more than held his own against one of Kilkenny's better players, Tommy Walsh while Kieran Murphy embellished a fine individual display with two points from play in the second half. Corcoran's second coming as a forward was unquestionably one of the primary reasons that Cork claimed ultimate honours after a long summer of hurling.

Cork's championship campaign began on May 16 at Páirc Uí Chaoimh with a 4-19 to 1-7 victory over Kerry and the Rebels then defeated Limerick in the Munster semi-final by 1-18 to 2-12. Cork came in for some severe criticism following their defeat by Waterford in a classic Munster final by a single point on a 3-16 to 1-21 scoreline but the Rebels answered their critics in the best possible manner with victories over Tipperary, Antrim and Wexford to reach the All-Ireland Final for the second successive year.

Cork's success owed much to the astute management of Donal O'Grady, who took over in December 2002 at what was an extremely difficult time after the players had gone on strike in protest at their treatment by the County Board. O'Grady proved to be the ideal manager and soon earned the respect of all the players. He guided the county to an All-Ireland Final appearance in 2003, which Cork narrowly lost to Kilkenny but it all came right against the same opposition last September when the Rebels moved to the top of the All-Ireland Roll of Honour with twenty-nine titles. However, O'Grady shocked Cork hurling just over three weeks later, early October 2004, when he stepped down from the position citing personal and business reasons for his decision.

ALL-IRELAND SENIOR HURLING CHAMPIONSHIP FINAL

CORK VERSUS KILKENNY
CROKE PARK
REFEREE: AODÁN MAC SUIBHNE (DUBLIN)
RESULT: CORK 0-17 KILKENNY 0-9

SCORERS – CORK: Joe Deane 0-5; Niall McCarthy 0-3; Ben O'Connor 0-3; Brian Corcoran 0-2; Kieran Murphy 0-2; Tom Kenny 0-1; Jerry O'Connor 0-1

SCORERS – KILKENNY: Henry Shefflin 0-5; Martin Comerford 0-2; Derek Lyng 0-1; James 'Cha' Fitzpatrick 0-1

CORK
Donal Óg Cusack

Wayne Sherlock   Diarmuid O'Sullivan   Brian Murphy

John Gardiner   Ronan Curran   Seán Óg Ó hAilpín

Tom Kenny   Jerry O'Connor

Ben O'Connor (*Captain*)   Niall McCarthy   Timmy McCarthy

Kieran Murphy   Brian Corcoran   Joe Deane

SUBSTITUTE: John Browne for Brian Murphy

KILKENNY
James McGarry

Michael Kavanagh   Noel Hickey   James Ryall

Tommy Walsh   Peter Barry   J.J. Delaney

Derek Lyng   Ken Coogan

Henry Shefflin   John Hoyne   D.J. Carey

James 'Cha' Fitzpatrick   Martin Comerford (*Captain*)   Eddie Brennan

SUBSTITUTES: Conor Phelan for James 'Cha' Fitzpatrick;
Seán Dowling for Ken Coogan

Ben O'Connor, Cork

Tommy Walsh, Kilkenny

erry O'Connor, Cork

Adrian Fenlon, Wexford

8th August, Croke Park:
Kilkenny 3–12   Waterford 0-18

15th August, Croke Park:
Cork 1–27   Wexford 0-12

Damien Fitzhenry, Wexford

J.J. Delaney, Kilkenny

ALL-IRELAND SENIOR HURLING CHAMPIONSHIP SEMI-FINAL

KILKENNY VERSUS WATERFORD
CROKE PARK
REFEREE: AODÁN MAC SUIBHNE (DUBLIN)
RESULT: KILKENNY 3-12 WATERFORD 0-18

SCORERS – KILKENNY: Henry Shefflin 2-4; Eddie Brennan 1-1; Martin Comerford 0-3; D.J. Carey 0-2; James 'Cha' Fitzpatrick 0-1; Ken Coogan 0-1

SCORERS – WATERFORD: Paul Flynn 0-13; Jack Kennedy 0-3; Michael Walsh 0-1; Eoin Kelly 0-1

KILKENNY
James McGarry

Michael Kavanagh   Noel Hickey   James Ryall

Tommy Walsh   Peter Barry   J.J. Delaney

Derek Lyng   Ken Coogan

Eddie Brennan   John Hoyne   D.J. Carey

James 'Cha' Fitzpatrick   Martin Comerford (*Captain*)   Henry Shefflin

SUBSTITUTES: None

WATERFORD
Ian O'Regan

Eoin Murphy   Declan Prendergast   James Murray

Tony Browne   Ken McGrath (*Captain*)   Brian Phelan

Dave Bennett   Eoin Kelly

Dan Shanahan   Michael Walsh   Paul Flynn

Shane O'Sullivan   Seamus Prendergast   Eoin McGrath

SUBSTITUTES: Jack Kennedy for Shane O'Sullivan; Paul O'Brien for Eoin McGrath

ALL-IRELAND SENIOR HURLING CHAMPIONSHIP SEMI-FINAL

CORK VERSUS WEXFORD
CROKE PARK
REFEREE: BARRY KELLY (WESTMEATH)
RESULT: CORK 1-27   WEXFORD 0-12

SCORERS – CORK: Ben O'Connor 0-8; Jerry O'Connor 0-6; Joe Deane 0-4; Tom Kenny 1-1; Timmy McCarthy 0-2; Niall McCarthy 0-2; Jonathan O'Callaghan 0-2; Kieran Murphy 0-1; Mickey O'Connell 0-1

SCORERS – WEXFORD: Declan Ruth 0-2; Tomás 'Mossy' Mahon 0-2; Paul Carley 0-2; Paul Codd 0-2; Mitch Jordan 0-2; Eoin Quigley 0-1; Malachy Travers 0-1

CORK
Donal Óg Cusack

Wayne Sherlock   Diarmuid O'Sullivan   Brian Murphy

Seán Óg Ó hAilpín   Ronan Curran   Cian O'Connor

Tom Kenny   Jerry O'Connor

Ben O'Connor (*Captain*)   Niall McCarthy   Timmy McCarthy

Kieran Murphy   Brian Corcoran   Joe Deane

SUBSTITUTES: Jonathan O'Callaghan for Joe Deane; John Paul King for Timmy McCarthy; Mickey O'Connell for Jerry O'Connor; John Browne for Wayne Sherlock; Pat Mulcahy for Diarmuid O'Sullivan

WEXFORD
Damien Fitzhenry

Malachy Travers   Darragh Ryan   David 'Doc' O'Connor

John O'Connor (*Captain*)   Declan Ruth   Rory McCarthy

Adrian Fenlon   Tomás 'Mossy' Mahon

Paul Carley   Eoin Quigley   Paul Codd

Rory Jacob   Michael Jacob   Mitch Jordan

SUBSTITUTES: Keith Rossiter for John O'Connor; Diarmuid Lyng for Tomás 'Mossy' Mahon; Larry Murphy for Michael Jacob; Chris 'Hopper' McGrath for Paul Carley; Barry Lambert for Eoin Quigley

Brian Corcoran, Cork

25th July, Croke Park:
Cork 2-26 Antrim 0-10

25th July Croke Park:
Kilkenny 1-13 Clare 1-13 (A draw)

31st July, Semple Stadium:
Kilkenny 1-11 Clare 0-9 (Replay)

Seán Óg Ó hAilpín, Cork

ALL-IRELAND SENIOR HURLING CHAMPIONSHIP QUARTER-FINAL

CORK VERSUS ANTRIM
CROKE PARK
REFEREE: AODÁN MAC SUIBHNE (DUBLIN)
RESULT: CORK 2-26 ANTRIM 0-10

SCORERS – CORK: Brian Corcoran 2-1; Joe Deane 0-4; Jonathan O'Callaghan 0-4; Jerry O'Connor 0-4; Ben O'Connor 0-3; Niall McCarthy 0-2; Timmy McCarthy 0-2; Mickey O'Connell 0-2; John Anderson 0-2; Kieran Murphy 0-1; John Gardiner 0-1

SCORERS – ANTRIM: Brian McFall 0-4; Paddy Richmond 0-3; Michael McCambridge 0-1; Colm McGuckian 0-1; Darren Quinn 0-1

CORK
Donal Óg Cusack

Wayne Sherlock   Diarmuid O'Sullivan   Brian Murphy

John Gardiner   Ronan Curran   Seán Óg Ó hAilpín

Tom Kenny   Jerry O'Connor

Ben O'Connor (*Captain*)   Niall McCarthy   Timmy McCarthy

Kieran Murphy   Brian Corcoran   Joe Deane

SUBSTITUTES: Mickey O'Connell for Jerry O'Connor; Jonathan O'Callaghan for Ben O'Connor; Cian O'Connor for Seán Óg Ó hAilpín; John Anderson for Niall McCarthy; John Browne for Diarmuid O'Sullivan

ANTRIM
D.D. Quinn

Mickey Kettle   Kieran Kelly   Brendan Herron

Michael McCambridge   Karl McKeegan   Johnny Campbell

Jim Connolly   Michael Magill

Michael Herron   Colm McGuckian (*Captain*)   Liam Richmond

Liam Watson   Paddy Richmond   Brian McFall

SUBSTITUTES: Darren Quinn for Liam Richmond; John McIntosh for Johnny Campbell; Martin Scullion for Jim Connolly; Gerard Cunningham for Michael McCambridge

ALL-IRELAND SENIOR HURLING CHAMPIONSHIP QUARTER-FINAL

KILKENNY VERSUS CLARE
CROKE PARK
REFEREE: GER HARRINGTON (CORK)
RESULT: KILKENNY 1-13 CLARE 1-13 (A DRAW)

SCORERS – KILKENNY: Henry Shefflin 0-9; John Hoyne 1-0; Jimmy Coogan 0-1; D.J. Carey 0-1; Pat Tennyson 0-1; Seán Dowling 0-1

SCORERS – CLARE: Niall Gilligan 1-7; Seánie McMahon 0-3; Andrew Quinn 0-1; Diarmuid McMahon 0-1; Jamesie O'Connor 0-1

KILKENNY
James McGarry

James Ryall   Noel Hickey   Tommy Walsh

Richie Mullally   Peter Barry   J.J. Delaney

Derek Lyng   Ken Coogan

Martin Comerford (*Captain*)   Henry Shefflin   Pat Tennyson

Eddie Brennan   D.J. Carey   Jimmy Coogan

SUBSTITUTES: John Hoyne for Eddie Brennan; Seán Dowling for Pat Tennyson; Paddy Mullally for Richie Mullally

CLARE
Davy Fitzgerald

Brian Quinn   Frank Lohan   Gerry O'Grady

David Hoey   Seánie McMahon (*Captain*)   Alan Markham

Colin Lynch   Diarmuid McMahon

Andrew Quinn   Gerry Quinn   David Forde

Niall Gilligan   Tony Griffin   Tony Carmody

SUBSTITUTES: Jamesie O'Connor for David Forde; Ollie Baker for Andrew Quinn; Daithí O'Connell for Diarmuid McMahon

ALL-IRELAND SENIOR HURLING CHAMPIONSHIP
QUARTER-FINAL REPLAY

KILKENNY VERSUS CLARE
SEMPLE STADIUM (THURLES)
REFEREE: PAT HORAN (OFFALY)
RESULT: KILKENNY 1-11 CLARE 0-9

SCORERS – KILKENNY: Eddie Brennan 1-2; Henry Shefflin 0-3; D.J. Carey 0-3; Martin Comerford 0-2; John Hoyne 0-1

SCORERS – CLARE: Niall Gilligan 0-3; Seánie McMahon 0-2; Jamesie O'Connor 0-2; David Forde 0-1; Tony Griffin 0-1

KILKENNY
James McGarry

Michael Kavanagh   Noel Hickey   James Ryall

Tommy Walsh   Peter Barry   J.J. Delaney

Derek Lyng   Ken Coogan

Eddie Brennan   John Hoyne   D.J. Carey

Martin Comerford (*Captain*)   Henry Shefflin   James 'Cha' Fitzpatrick

SUBSTITUTES: John Maher for Henry Shefflin; Seán Dowling for Ken Coogan

CLARE
Davy Fitzgerald

Brian Quinn   Brian Lohan   Gerry O'Grady

David Hoey   Seánie McMahon (*Captain*)   Frank Lohan

Diarmuid McMahon   Colin Lynch

John Reddan   Gerry Quinn   Andrew Quinn

Niall Gilligan   Tony Griffin   Alan Markham

SUBSTITUTES: Conor Plunkett for Brian Lohan; Jamesie O'Connor for Andrew Quinn; David Forde for David Hoey; Barry Murphy for John Reddan; Ollie Baker for Alan Markham

FIRST ROUND:

16th May, Semple Stadium:
Waterford 3- 21   Clare 1- 8

16th May, Páirc Uí Chaoimh:
Cork 4-19   Kerry 1-7

SEMI-FINALS

30th May, Gaelic Grounds:
Cork 1-18   Limerick 2-12

6th June, Páirc Ui Chaoimh:
Waterford 4-10   Tipperary 3-12

FINAL:

27th June, Semple Stadium:
Waterford 3-16   Cork 1-21

Paul Flynn, Waterford

Dan Shanahan, Waterford

MUNSTER SENIOR HURLING CHAMPIONSHIP FIRST ROUND

WATERFORD VERSUS CLARE
SEMPLE STADIUM (THURLES)
REFEREE: GER HARRINGTON (CORK)
RESULT: WATERFORD 3-21 CLARE 1-8

SCORERS – WATERFORD: Dan Shanahan 3-1; Eoin Kelly 0-8; Dave Bennett 0-5; John Mullane 0-4; Seamus Prendergast 0-1; Paul Flynn 0-1; Michael Walsh 0-1

SCORERS – CLARE: Niall Gilligan 0-4; Frank Lohan 0-3; Tony Griffin 1-0; Colin Lynch 0-1

WATERFORD
Stephen Brenner

Eoin Murphy   Tom Feeney   James Murray

Tony Browne   Ken McGrath (*Captain*)   Brian Phelan

Dave Bennett   Eoin Kelly

Dan Shanahan   Michael Walsh   Paul Flynn

John Mullane   Seamus Prendergast   Eoin McGrath

SUBSTITUTES: Paul O'Brien for Paul Flynn; Seán Ryan for Eoin McGrath; Andy Moloney for Seamus Prendergast

CLARE
Davy Fitzgerald

Brian Quinn   Brian Lohan   Brian O'Connell

Gerry Quinn   Seánie McMahon (*Captain*)   Conor Plunkett

Ollie Baker   Diarmuid McMahon

Tony Griffin   Colin Lynch   Alan Markham

Niall Gilligan   Frank Lohan   David Forde

SUBSTITUTES: Tony Carmody for Ollie Baker; David Hoey for Brian O'Connell; Jamesie O'Connor for Alan Markham; Daithí O'Connell for Jamesie O'Connor; Colin Forde for Gerry Quinn

SUNDAY, MAY 16, 2004

MUNSTER SENIOR HURLING CHAMPIONSHIP FIRST ROUND

CORK VERSUS KERRY
PÁIRC UÍ CHAOIMH (CORK)
REFEREE: BARRY KELLY (WESTMEATH)
RESULT: CORK 4-19 KERRY 1-7

SCORERS – CORK: Joe Deane 1-4; John Gardiner 1-1; Ben O'Connor 1-1; Brian Corcoran 1-1; Jerry O'Connor 0-3; Mickey O'Connell 0-2; Niall McCarthy 0-2; Jonathan O'Callaghan 0-2; Ronan Curran 0-1; John Anderson 0-1; Timmy McCarthy 0-1

SCORERS – KERRY: Errol Tuohy 1-1; Shane Brick 0-2; Pat O'Connell 0-2; James McCarthy 0-1; John Egan 0-1

CORK
Donal Óg Cusack

Brian Murphy   Diarmuid O'Sullivan   Cian O'Connor

Tom Kenny   Ronan Curran   Seán Óg Ó hAilpín

John Gardiner   Mickey O'Connell

Jerry O'Connor   Niall McCarthy   Timmy McCarthy

Ben O'Connor (*Captain*)   Joe Deane   Jonathan O'Callaghan

SUBSTITUTES: John Anderson for Niall McCarthy; Brian Corcoran for Joe Deane; Paul Tierney for John Gardiner; John Browne for Tom Kenny; Brendan Lombard for Jonathan O'Callaghan

KERRY
Tadhg Flynn

Brendan Blackwell   Aidan Healy   Andrew Keane

Kieran O'Sullivan   James McCarthy   Colin Harris

Aidan Cronin   Darren Young

Ivan McCarthy   Shane Brick (*Captain*)   Pat O'Connell

Errol Tuohy   John Mike Dooley   John Egan

SUBSTITUTES: Liam Boyle for Darren Young; Michael Lucid for Ivan McCarthy

SUNDAY, MAY 30, 2004

MUNSTER SENIOR HURLING CHAMPIONSHIP SEMI-FINAL

CORK VERSUS LIMERICK
GAELIC GROUNDS (LIMERICK)
REFEREE: SEAMUS ROCHE (TIPPERARY)
RESULT: CORK 1-18   LIMERICK 2-12

SCORERS – CORK: Ben O'Connor 1-7; Joe Deane 0-4; Niall McCarthy 0-3; Timmy McCarthy 0-1; Brian Corcoran 0-1; Mickey O'Connell 0-1; Jerry O'Connor 0-1

SCORERS – LIMERICK: Niall Moran 0-7; Seán O'Connor 2-0; Pat Tobin 0-2; Michael McKenna 0-1; John Paul Sheahan 0-1; Donnacha Sheehan 0-1

CORK
Donal Óg Cusack
Wayne Sherlock   Diarmuid O'Sullivan   Brian Murphy
Tom Kenny   Ronan Curran   Seán Óg Ó hAilpín
John Gardiner   Mickey O'Connell
Niall McCarthy   Jerry O'Connor   Timmy McCarthy
Jonathan O'Callaghan   Ben O'Connor (*Captain*)   Joe Deane

SUBSTITUTES: Brian Corcoran for Timmy McCarthy; Michael Byrne for Jonathan O'Callaghan

LIMERICK
Albert Shanahan
Damien Reale   T.J. Ryan (*Captain*)   Mickey Cahill
Ollie Moran   Brian Geary   Peter Lawlor
Clem Smith   Mark Foley
Niall Moran   John Paul Sheahan   Michael McKenna
Andrew O'Shaughnessy   Seán O'Connor   Donnacha Sheehan

SUBSTITUTES: Pat Tobin for John Paul Sheahan; Donal O'Grady for Donnacha Sheehan

Diarmuid O'Sullivan, Cork

Tony Browne, Waterford

SUNDAY, JUNE 6, 2004

MUNSTER SENIOR HURLING CHAMPIONSHIP SEMI-FINAL

WATERFORD VERSUS TIPPERARY
PÁIRC UÍ CHAOIMH (CORK)
REFEREE: DIARMUID KIRWAN (CORK)
RESULT: WATERFORD 4-10   TIPPERARY 3-12

SCORERS – WATERFORD: Dan Shanahan 2-0; John Mullane 1-0; Paul O'Brien 1-0; Dave Bennett 0-2; Paul Flynn 0-2; Seamus Prendergast 0-2; Eoin Kelly 0-2; Michael Walsh 0-1; Eoin McGrath 0-1

SCORERS – TIPPERARY: Eoin Kelly 2-8; Colin Morrissey 1-1; Paul Kelly 0-1; Tommy Dunne 0-1; Seamus Butler 0-1

WATERFORD
Stephen Brenner

James Murray   Declan Prendergast   Brian Wall

Brian Phelan   Ken McGrath (*Captain*)   Eoin Murphy

Dave Bennett   Eoin Kelly

Dan Shanahan   Michael Walsh   Paul Flynn

John Mullane   Seamus Prendergast   Eoin McGrath

SUBSTITUTES: Paul O'Brien for Eoin McGrath; Shane O'Sullivan for Paul Flynn; Tom Feeney for Ken McGrath

TIPPERARY
Brendan Cummins

Thomas Costello   Philip Maher   Paul Curran

Paul Kelly   Diarmuid Fitzgerald   Eamonn Corcoran

Eddie Enright   Colin Morrissey

Tommy Dunne (*Captain*)   John Carroll   Benny Dunne

Eoin Kelly   John Devane   Paddy O'Brien

SUBSTITUTES: Seamus Butler for Paddy O'Brien; Martin Maher for Thomas Costello; Conor Gleeson for John Carroll; Mark O'Leary for Benny Dunne

MUNSTER SENIOR HURLING CHAMPIONSHIP FINAL

WATERFORD VERSUS CORK
SEMPLE STADIUM (THURLES)
REFEREE: SEÁN MCMAHON (CLARE)
RESULT: WATERFORD 3-16 CORK 1-21

SCORERS – WATERFORD: Paul Flynn 1-7; Dan Shanahan 1-3; Eoin Kelly 1-1; John Mullane 0-2; Seamus Prendergast 0-1; Dave Bennett 0-1; Ken McGrath 0-1

SCORERS – CORK: Joe Deane 0-9; Ben O'Connor 0-4; Garvan McCarthy 1-0; Tom Kenny 0-3; Jerry O'Connor 0-2; Brian Corcoran 0-2; Ronan Curran 0-1

WATERFORD
Stephen Brenner

James Murray Declan Prendergast Eoin Murphy

Tony Browne Ken McGrath (*Captain*) Brian Phelan

Dave Bennett Eoin Kelly

Dan Shanahan Michael Walsh Paul Flynn

John Mullane Seamus Prendergast Eoin McGrath

SUBSTITUTES: Paul O'Brien for Dave Bennett; Shane O'Sullivan for Eoin McGrath; Jack Kennedy for Paul O'Brien

CORK
Donal Óg Cusack

Wayne Sherlock Diarmuid O'Sullivan Brian Murphy

Seán Óg Ó hAilpín Ronan Curran John Gardiner

Tom Kenny Jerry O'Connor

Garvan McCarthy Niall McCarthy Timmy McCarthy

Ben O'Connor (*Captain*) Brian Corcoran Joe Deane

SUBSTITUTES: Jonathan O'Callaghan for Niall McCarthy; Kieran Murphy for Garvan McCarthy; Cian O'Connor for John Gardiner

Ken McGrath, Waterford

Joe Deane, Cork

Conal Keaney, Dublin

FIRST ROUND:

2nd May, Cusack Park:
Westmeath 6-14   Wicklow 1-13

2nd May, Dr. Cullen Park:
Laois 4-19   Carlow 0-8

16th May, Cusack Park:
Westmeath 1-18   Kildare 1-6

16th May, O'Moore Park:
Laois 1-13   Meath 0-8

QUARTER-FINALS:

29th May, O'Connor Park:
Offaly 2-23   Laois 1-15

13th June, Croke Park:
Dublin 2-14   Westmeath 0-11

SEMI-FINALS:

13th June, Croke Park:
Wexford 2-15   Kilkenny 1-16

20th June, Croke Park:
Offaly 2-25   Dublin 1-13

FINAL:

4th July, Croke Park:
Wexford 2-12   Offaly 1-11

LEINSTER SENIOR HURLING CHAMPIONSHIP FIRST ROUND

WESTMEATH VERSUS WICKLOW
CUSACK PARK (MULLINGAR)
REFEREE: FERGUS SMITH (MEATH)
RESULT: WESTMEATH 6-14 WICKLOW 1-13

SCORERS – WESTMEATH: Andrew Mitchell 1-8; John Shaw 2-1; Ronan Whelan 1-2; Vincent Bateman 1-0; Frank Shaw 1-0; Barry Kennedy 0-1; Derek Gallagher 0-1; Brian Connaughton 0-1

SCORERS – WICKLOW: Jonathan O'Neill 1-11; Trevor McGrath 0-1; Gary Doran 0-1

WESTMEATH
Mark Briody

Dermot Curley　　Brendan Murtagh　　Paul Greville

Derek Gallagher　　Christo Murtagh　　Darren McCormack (*Captain*)

Paul Williams　　Ollie Devine

Ronan Whelan　　Vincent Bateman　　Andrew Mitchell

Daniel Carty　　John Shaw　　Barry Kennedy

SUBSTITUTES: Brian Connaughton for Paul Williams; Frank Shaw for Barry Kennedy; Shane McDonnell for Ollie Devine; Killian Cosgrove for Daniel Carty; Donal Devine for Andrew Mitchell

WICKLOW
Thomas Finn

Michael John O'Neill　　Graham Keogh　　Jeffrey Bermingham

Seán Kinsella　　Michael Anthony O'Neill (*Captain*)　　Trevor McGrath

Christy O'Toole　　Gerry Murray

Joe Murphy　　Gary Doran　　Christopher Kavanagh

Alan Tiernan　　Jonathan O'Neill　　David Moran

SUBSTITUTES: Diarmuid Doran for Seán Kinsella; Denis Moran for Alan Tiernan; John Sinnott for David Moran

LEINSTER SENIOR HURLING CHAMPIONSHIP FIRST ROUND

LAOIS VERSUS CARLOW
DR. CULLEN PARK (CARLOW)
REFEREE: EAMONN MORRIS (DUBLIN)
RESULT: LAOIS 4-19 CARLOW 0-8

SCORERS – LAOIS: Tommy Fitzgerald 1-3; Paul Cuddy 0-5; Enda Meagher 0-3; Damien Culleton 1-0; Eamonn Jackman 1-0; Eoin Browne 1-0; Darren Rooney 0-2; Damien Walsh 0-2; Fran Keenan 0-2; James Walsh 0-1; Joe Fitzpatrick 0-1

SCORERS – CARLOW: Pat Coady 0-4; Karl English 0-2; Seán Michael Murphy 0-1; Frank Foley 0-1

LAOIS
Kevin Galvin

Cyril Cuddy   Pakie Cuddy   Michael McEvoy

Joe Fitzpatrick   Paul Cuddy (*Captain*)   Rory Conroy

Darren Rooney   James Walsh

Canice Coonan   Fran Keenan   Enda Meagher

Tommy Fitzgerald   Liam Tynan   Damien Culleton

SUBSTITUTES: Eoin Browne for Canice Coonan; Alan Delaney for Joe Fitzpatrick; Cathal Brophy for James Walsh; Eamonn Jackman for Fran Keenan; Damien Walsh for Liam Tynan

CARLOW
Frank Foley

Willie Hickey   Adrian Corcoran   Michael Kehoe

Kenneth Nolan   Edward Coady   Andrew Gaul

Shane Kavanagh   Pat Coady

Paul Kehoe   Dessie Murphy (*Captain*)   Ronan Minchin

Brian Murphy   Karl English   Seamus Smithers

SUBSTITUTES: Seán Michael Murphy for Shane Kavanagh; Dessie Shaw for Michael Kehoe; Tommy O'Shea for Seamus Smithers; Paddy Coady for Brian Murphy; Stephen Shiel for Andrew Gaul

LEINSTER SENIOR HURLING CHAMPIONSHIP FIRST ROUND

WESTMEATH VERSUS KILDARE
CUSACK PARK (MULLINGAR)
REFEREE: JOHN GUINAN (KILKENNY)
RESULT: WESTMEATH 1-18 KILDARE 1-6

SCORERS – WESTMEATH: Andrew Mitchell 0-9; Jonathan Forbes 1-2;
Barry Kennedy 0-3; Ollie Devine 0-2; Darren McCormack 0-2

SCORERS – KILDARE: Joe Dempsey 1-1; Tom Carew 0-3; Andy Quinn 0-1;
Ciaran Divilly 0-1

WESTMEATH
Mark Briody

Dermot Curley   Brendan Murtagh   Paul Greville

Derek Gallagher   Darren McCormack (*Captain*)   Shane McDonnell

Ronan Whelan   Brian Connaughton

Killian Cosgrove   Ollie Devine   Andrew Mitchell

Derek McNicholas   John Shaw   Barry Kennedy

SUBSTITUTES: Daniel Carty for Derek McNicholas;
Jonathan Forbes for Killian Cosgrove; Christo Murtagh for Daniel Carty;
Paul Williams for Brian Connaughton; Niall Flanagan for John Shaw;
Christy Fanning for Ollie Devine

KILDARE
Cormac Leahy

Stephen Crowe   Darragh Lahart   Brendan Maher

Ciarán Divilly   David Harney   Richie Hoban

Colm Buggy   John Brennan

Joe Dempsey   Eamonn Denieffe   Shane Joyce

Adrian McAndrew (*Captain*)   Andy Quinn   Tom Carew

SUBSTITUTES: Billy White for Shane Joyce; Paudie Reidy for Brendan Maher;
Alan Flaherty for Stephen Crowe; Peter Beirne for David Harney;
Conal Boran for Eamonn Denieffe

LEINSTER SENIOR HURLING CHAMPIONSHIP FIRST ROUND

LAOIS VERSUS MEATH
O'MOORE PARK (PORTLAOISE)
REFEREE: JOE KELLY (WEXFORD)
RESULT: LAOIS 1–13 MEATH 0–8

SCORERS – LAOIS: James Young 1-6; Robert Jones 0-4; Enda Meagher 0-1; Tommy Fitzgerald 0-1; Paul Cuddy 0-1

SCORERS – MEATH: Mickey Cole 0-3; Eibhin Lynam 0-2; Seán Reilly 0-1; Stephen Clynch 0-1; Mark Gannon 0-1

LAOIS
Kevin Galvin
Cyril Cuddy   Pakie Cuddy   Michael McEvoy
Joe Fitzpatrick   Paul Cuddy (*Captain*)   Rory Conroy
Darren Rooney   James Walsh
Robert Jones   James Young   Enda Meagher
Tommy Fitzgerald   Liam Tynan   Damien Culleton

SUBSTITUTES: Jimmy Dunne for Darren Rooney; Pat Mahon for James Walsh; Eoin Browne for Enda Meagher; Cathal Brophy for Tommy Fitzgerald

MEATH
Mark Brennan
Seán White   Pat Roche   Seán Moran
Diarmuid Brennan   Thomas Reilly   Seán Reilly
Jimmy Canty   David Donnelly
Eibhin Lynam   Stephen Clynch   Michael Burke
Neville Reilly   Mark Gannon   Tony Fox (*Captain*)

SUBSTITUTES: Mickey Cole for Michael Burke; Joey Keena for Jimmy Canty; Padraig Donoghue for Seán Moran; Ger O'Neill for Tony Fox

Eibhin Lynam, Meath

James Young, Laois

LEINSTER SENIOR HURLING CHAMPIONSHIP QUARTER-FINAL

OFFALY VERSUS LAOIS
O'CONNOR PARK (TULLAMORE)
REFEREE: SEÁN MCMAHON (CLARE)
RESULT: OFFALY 2-23 LAOIS 1-15

SCORERS – OFFALY: Damien Murray 0-10; Brian Carroll 1-4; Brendan Murphy 1-2; Colm Cassidy 0-3; Michael Cordial 0-1; Simon Whelahan 0-1: Gary Hanniffy 0-1; Joe Brady 0-1

SCORERS – LAOIS: James Young 0-11; Canice Coonan 1-0; Robert Jones 0-1; Joe Fitzpatrick 0-1; Damien Culleton 0-1; David Cuddy 0-1

OFFALY
Brian Mullins

Mick O'Hara   Ger Oakley   David Franks

Kevin Brady   Niall Claffey   Colm Cassidy

Michael Cordial   Barry Whelahan

Neville Coughlan   Gary Hanniffy (*Captain*)   Brendan Murphy

Brian Carroll   Joe Brady   Damien Murray

SUBSTITUTES: Simon Whelahan for Joe Brady; Dylan Hayden for Barry Whelahan

LAOIS
Kevin Galvin

Cyril Cuddy   Darren Rooney   Michael McEvoy

Joe Fitzpatrick   Paul Cuddy   Rory Conroy

David Cuddy (*Captain*)   James Walsh

Canice Coonan   James Young   Robert Jones

Tommy Fitzgerald   Liam Tynan   Damien Culleton

SUBSTITUTES: Enda Meagher for James Walsh; Cathal Brophy for Rory Conroy; Jimmy Dunne for Robert Jones; Fran Keenan for Enda Meagher

LEINSTER SENIOR HURLING CHAMPIONSHIP QUARTER-FINAL

DUBLIN VERSUS WESTMEATH
CROKE PARK
REFEREE: DIARMUID KIRWAN (CORK)
RESULT: DUBLIN 2-14 WESTMEATH 0-11

SCORERS – DUBLIN: Conal Keaney 1-2; David O'Callaghan 1-1; David Curtin 0-3; Padraig Fleury 0-2; Liam Ryan 0-2; Johnny McGuirk 0-1; Kevin Flynn 0-1; Seán O'Shea 0-1; Michael Carton 0-1

SCORERS – WESTMEATH: Andrew Mitchell 0-5; Enda Loughlin 0-2; Ronan Whelan 0-1; Killian Cosgrove 0-1; Vincent Bateman 0-1; John Shaw 0-1

DUBLIN
Gary Maguire
Darragh Spain   Simon Daly   Aodhán de Paor
Stephen Hiney   Ronan Fallon   Kevin Ryan
Carl Meehan   Conal Keaney
David Curtin   Liam Ryan   Michael Carton
David O'Callaghan   Kevin Flynn (*Captain*)   David Donnelly

SUBSTITUTES: Padraig Fleury for David Donnelly; Johnny McGuirk for David Curtin; Seán O'Shea for Carl Meehan; Seán McCann for Michael Carton

WESTMEATH
Mark Briody
Dermot Curley   Christo Murtagh   Paul Greville
Ollie Devine   Brendan Murtagh   Darren McCormack (*Captain*)
Ronan Whelan   Enda Loughlin
Jonathan Forbes   Vincent Bateman   Andrew Mitchell
Daniel Carty   Killian Cosgrove   John Shaw

SUBSTITUTES: Barry Kennedy for Jonathan Forbes; Niall Flanagan for Daniel Carty; Shane McDonnell for Killian Cosgrove; Derek Gallagher for Niall Flanagan; Paul Williams for Barry Kennedy

LEINSTER SENIOR HURLING CHAMPIONSHIP SEMI-FINAL

WEXFORD VERSUS KILKENNY
CROKE PARK
REFEREE: BARRY KELLY (WESTMEATH)
RESULT: WEXFORD 2-15 KILKENNY 1-16

SCORERS – WEXFORD: Michael Jacob 1-2; Barry Lambert 0-4; Rory Jacob 1-1; Paul Carley 0-3; Mitch Jordan 0-3; Adrian Fenlon 0-1; Eoin Quigley 0-1

SCORERS – KILKENNY: Henry Shefflin 0-5; Eddie Brennan 1-1; Tommy Walsh 0-2; Martin Comerford 0-2; Seán Dowling 0-2; Pat Tennyson 0-1; John Hoyne 0-1; D.J. Carey 0-1; Jimmy Coogan 0-1

WEXFORD
Damien Fitzhenry

David 'Doc' O'Connor   Darragh Ryan   Malachy Travers

John O'Connor (*Captain*)   Declan Ruth   Rory McCarthy

Adrian Fenlon   Tomás 'Mossy' Mahon

Barry Lambert   Eoin Quigley   Paul Carley

Mitch Jordan   Michael Jacob   Rory Jacob

SUBSTITUTES: Larry Murphy for Barry Lambert; Paul Codd for Tomás 'Mossy' Mahon; Colm Kehoe for Darragh Ryan

KILKENNY
James McGarry

Michael Kavanagh   Noel Hickey   J.J. Delaney

Seán Dowling   Peter Barry   Brian Hogan

Derek Lyng   Pat Tennyson

John Hoyne   Henry Shefflin   Tommy Walsh

Eddie Brennan   Martin Comerford (*Captain*)   Jimmy Coogan

SUBSTITUTES: D.J. Carey for Jimmy Coogan; Aidan Fogarty for John Hoyne

LEINSTER SENIOR HURLING CHAMPIONSHIP SEMI-FINAL

OFFALY VERSUS DUBLIN
CROKE PARK
REFEREE: PAT AHERN (CARLOW)
RESULT: OFFALY 2-25 DUBLIN 1-13

SCORERS – OFFALY: Brendan Murphy 2-5; Damien Murray 0-8; Brian Carroll 0-4; Rory Hanniffy 0-3; Michael Cordial 0-3; Colm Cassidy 0-2

SCORERS – DUBLIN: David O'Callaghan 0-5; Michael Carton 1-0; Liam Ryan 0-2; Aodhán De Paor 0-2; Kevin Flynn 0-2; David Kirwan 0-1; David Sweeney 0-1

OFFALY
Brian Mullins

Barry Teehan   Ger Oakley   David Franks

Niall Claffey   Brian Whelahan   Colm Cassidy

Michael Cordial   Barry Whelahan

Gary Hanniffy (*Captain*)   Rory Hanniffy   Brendan Murphy

Brian Carroll   Joe Brady   Damien Murray

SUBSTITUTES: Kevin Brady for David Franks; Neville Coughlan for Michael Cordial; Simon Whelahan for Joe Brady

DUBLIN
Gary Maguire

Darragh Spain   Stephen Perkins   Simon Daly

Aodhán De Paor   Ronan Fallon   Kevin Ryan

Carl Meehan   Johnny McGuirk

David Sweeney   Liam Ryan   Kevin Flynn (*Captain*)

David O'Callaghan   Stephen Hiney   Padraig Fleury

SUBSTITUTES: David Kirwan for Carl Meehan; Michael Carton for Johnny McGuirk; Philly Brennan for Darragh Spain; Derek O'Reilly for Stephen Perkins; Seán O'Shea for Ronan Fallon

LEINSTER SENIOR HURLING CHAMPIONSHIP FINAL

WEXFORD VERSUS OFFALY
CROKE PARK
REFEREE: GER HARRINGTON (CORK)
RESULT: WEXFORD 2-12 OFFALY 1-11

SCORERS – WEXFORD: Paul Carley 1-1; Barry Lambert 0-3; Eoin Quigley 0-3;
Michael Jacob 1-0; Paul Codd 0-2; Rory Jacob 0-2; Adrian Fenlon 0-1

SCORERS – OFFALY: Damien Murray 0-4; Gary Hanniffy 1-0; Brian Carroll 0-2;
Brendan Murphy 0-1; Michael Cordial 0-1; Rory Hanniffy 0-1; Colm Cassidy 0-1;
Barry Whelahan 0-1

WEXFORD

Damien Fitzhenry

Malachy Travers   Darragh Ryan   David 'Doc' O'Connor

Rory McCarthy   Declan Ruth   John O'Connor (*Captain*)

Adrian Fenlon   Tomás 'Mossy' Mahon

Paul Carley   Eoin Quigley   Barry Lambert

Mitch Jordan   Michael Jacob   Rory Jacob

SUBSTITUTES: Paul Codd for Barry Lambert; Chris 'Hopper' McGrath for Mitch Jordan

OFFALY

Brian Mullins

Barry Teehan   Ger Oakley   David Franks

Niall Claffey   Brian Whelahan   Colm Cassidy

Michael Cordial   Barry Whelahan

Gary Hanniffy (*Captain*)   Rory Hanniffy   Brendan Murphy

Brian Carroll   Joe Brady   Damien Murray

SUBSTITUTES: Neville Coughlan for Brian Whelahan;
Stephen Brown for Brian Carroll; Dylan Hayden for Joe Brady

Above: Rory Hanniffy, Offaly
Below: Brian Whelahan, Offaly

Brian McFall, Antrim

FIRST ROUND:

16th May, Ruislip:
Derry 2-14   London 0-12

SEMI-FINALS:

23rd May, Casement Park:
Antrim 2-14   Derry 0-12

23rd May, Gaelic Park:
Down 1-19   New York 1-9

FINAL:

6th June, Casement Park:
Antrim 1-15   Down 1-15   (A Draw)

13th June, Casement Park:
Antrim 3-14   Down 0-18   (Replay)

ULSTER SENIOR HURLING CHAMPIONSHIP FIRST ROUND

DERRY VERSUS LONDON
RUISLIP (LONDON)
REFEREE: JOHN SEXTON (LIMERICK)
RESULT: DERRY 2-14 LONDON 0-12

SCORERS – DERRY: Geoffrey McGonigle 1-4; Danny McGrellis 0-3;
Gregory Biggs 0-3; Kevin Hinphey 1-0; Gary Biggs 0-2; Phelim Kelly 0-1;
Paul Hearty 0-1

SCORERS – LONDON: Dave Bourke 0-8; Mick Hayes 0-1; Fergus McMahon 0-1;
Teu Ó hAilpín 0-1; Eric Kinlon 0-1

DERRY
Kieran Stevenson

Gregory Brunton   Liam Hinphey   Michael Conway

Benny Ward   Cathal Brunton   Peter O'Kane

Ruairí Convery   Phelim Kelly

Kevin Hinphey   Gregory Biggs (*Captain*)   Gary Biggs

Danny McGrellis   Paul Hearty   Geoffrey McGonigle

SUBSTITUTE: Paul Doherty for Paul Hearty

LONDON
John Joe Burke

Stephen Dennehy   Mick Gordon (*Captain*)   Eamon Leamy

Shane Linnane   Brian Foley   Eamonn Phelan

Mick Hayes   Kevin Ivors

Dave Bourke   Nicholas Lalor   Fergus McMahon

Teu Ó hAilpín   Colm Buckley   Keith White

SUBSTITUTES: Niall Murphy for Colm Buckley; Colm Heaney for Shane Linnane;
Eric Kinlon for Nicholas Lalor; Michael O'Meara for Colm Heaney;
Tom Lalor for Eamon Leamy

ULSTER SENIOR HURLING CHAMPIONSHIP SEMI-FINAL

ANTRIM VERSUS DERRY
CASEMENT PARK (BELFAST)
REFEREE: BRIAN GAVIN (OFFALY)
RESULT: ANTRIM 2-14 DERRY 0-12

SCORERS – ANTRIM: Brian McFall 0-5; Jim Connolly 1-2; Liam Watson 0-3; Paddy Richmond 1-0; Karl McKeegan 0-1; Colm McGuckian 0-1; Michael Herron 0-1; Liam Richmond 0-1

SCORERS – DERRY: Gregory Biggs 0-5; Geoffrey McGonigle 0-3; Kevin Hinphey 0-2; Paul Doherty 0-1; Gary Biggs 0-1

ANTRIM
D.D. Quinn

Michael McCambridge   Kieran Kelly   Brendan Herron

Johnny Campbell   Karl McKeegan   Ciarán Herron

Jim Connolly   Martin Scullion

Liam Richmond   Colm McGuckian (*Captain*)   Michael Herron

Liam Watson   Paddy Richmond   Brian McFall

SUBSTITUTES: Darren Quinn for Liam Watson; John McIntosh for Martin Scullion

DERRY
Kieran Stevenson

Gregory Brunton   Liam Hinphey   Michael Conway

Benny Ward   Cathal Brunton   Peter O'Kane

Gary Biggs   Phelim Kelly

Kevin Hinphey   Gregory Biggs (*Captain*)   Geoffrey McGonigle

Danny McGrellis   Paul Hearty   Paul Doherty

SUBSTITUTES: Barry McGoldrick for Danny McGrellis;
Anton Rafferty for Cathal Brunton

ULSTER SENIOR HURLING CHAMPIONSHIP SEMI-FINAL

DOWN VERSUS NEW YORK
GAELIC PARK (NEW YORK)
REFEREE: PAT HORAN (OFFALY)
RESULT: DOWN 1-19   NEW YORK 1-9

SCORERS – DOWN: Paul Braniff 0-8; Gareth Johnson 1-1; Martin Coulter (Junior) 0-3; Brendan McGourty 0-2; Gerard Adair 0-2; Simon Wilson 0-1; Michael Braniff 0-1; Gerard McGrattan 0-1

SCORERS – NEW YORK: Bonny Kennedy 1-2; Vinny Norton 0-2; David Simms 0-2; Tom Moylan 0-2; Seán Quirke 0-1

DOWN
Graham Clarke

Liam Clarke   Stephen Murray   James Henry Hughes

Simon Wilson   Gary Savage   Gabriel Clarke

Andy Savage   Gerard Adair

Gerard McGrattan   Paul Braniff   Brendan McGourty

Martin Coulter (Junior) (*Captain*)   Gareth Johnson   Michael Braniff

SUBSTITUTES: John Convery for Andy Savage; Emmett Trainor for Paul Braniff; Ryan Conlon for Michael Braniff

NEW YORK
Kevin Jordan

Aidan Kiely   Peter Dalton   Philip Wickham

Seán Quirke (*Captain*)   John Madden   Tadhg O'Callaghan

Adrian Guinan   Seán Nolan

Bonny Kennedy   Vinny Norton   Trevor Fletcher

David Simms   Tom Moylan   Denis McCarthy

SUBSTITUTES: Gearóid O'Halloran for Denis McCarthy; Thomas Maher for David Simms; David Loughnane for Trevor Fletcher; Colin Ruth for Adrian Guinan

ULSTER SENIOR HURLING CHAMPIONSHIP FINAL

ANTRIM VERSUS DOWN
CASEMENT PARK (BELFAST)
REFEREE: MICHAEL HAVERTY (GALWAY)
RESULT: ANTRIM 1-15 DOWN 1-15 (A DRAW)

SCORERS – ANTRIM: Brian McFall 0-5; Darren Quinn 0-4; Michael Herron 1-1;
Paddy Richmond 0-3; Karl McKeegan 0-1; Colm McGuckian 0-1

SCORERS – DOWN: Gareth Johnson 0-4; Martin Coulter (Junior) 1-1;
Brendan McGourty 0-2; Simon Wilson 0-2; Stephen Clarke 0-2; John Convery 0-1;
Gerard McGrattan 0-1; Gerard Adair 0-1; Gary Savage 0-1

ANTRIM
D.D. Quinn

Gerard Cunningham   Kieran Kelly   Brendan Herron

Michael McCambridge   Karl McKeegan   Johnny Campbell

Ciarán Herron   Jim Connolly

Michael Herron   Colm McGuckian (*Captain*)   Liam Richmond

Darren Quinn   Paddy Richmond   Brian McFall

SUBSTITUTES: Liam Watson for Liam Richmond;
Mickey Kettle for Gerard Cunningham; John McIntosh for Jim Connolly

DOWN
Graham Clarke

Liam Clarke   Stephen Murray   James Henry Hughes

Simon Wilson   Gary Savage   Gabriel Clarke

Gerard Adair   Andy Savage

Gerard McGrattan   John Convery   Brendan McGourty

Martin Coulter (Junior) (*Captain*)   Gareth Johnson   Michael Braniff

SUBSTITUTES: Stephen Clarke for Michael Braniff;
Emmett Dorrian for James Henry Hughes; Emmett Trainor for Gerard McGrattan;
Eoin Clarke for Gareth Johnson

ULSTER SENIOR HURLING CHAMPIONSHIP FINAL REPLAY

ANTRIM VERSUS DOWN
CASEMENT PARK (BELFAST)
REFEREE: EAMONN MORRIS (DUBLIN)
RESULT: ANTRIM 3-14 DOWN 0-18

SCORERS – ANTRIM: Paddy Richmond 2-3; Brian McFall 1-3; Michael Herron 0-2; Liam Watson 0-2; Brendan Herron 0-1; Ciarán Herron 0-1; Jim Connolly 0-1; Colm McGuckian 0-1

SCORERS – DOWN: Stephen Clarke 0-6; Brendan McGourty 0-4; Gareth Johnson 0-2; John Convery 0-2; Simon Wilson 0-1; Gerard Adair 0-1; Andy Savage 0-1; Martin Coulter (Junior) 0-1

ANTRIM
D.D. Quinn

Mickey Kettle   Kieran Kelly   Brendan Herron

Michael McCambridge   Karl McKeegan   Johnny Campbell

Ciarán Herron   Jim Connolly

Michael Herron   Colm McGuckian (*Captain*)   Liam Watson

Darren Quinn   Paddy Richmond   Brian McFall

SUBSTITUTES: Liam Richmond for Michael McCambridge; John McIntosh for Liam Watson; Gareth Ward for Darren Quinn; Michael Magill for Jim Connolly

DOWN
Graham Clarke

Liam Clarke   Stephen Murray   Emmett Dorrian

Simon Wilson   Gary Savage   Gabriel Clarke

Gerard Adair   Andy Savage

Gerard McGrattan   John Convery   Brendan McGourty

Martin Coulter (Junior) (*Captain*)   Gareth Johnson   Stephen Clarke

SUBSTITUTES: James Henry Hughes for Simon Wilson; Paddy Hughes for Stephen Murray; Andrew Bell for James Henry Hughes

19th June, O'Moore Park:
Laois 3-13   Westmeath 4-5

26th June, Gaelic Grounds:
Clare 7-19   Laois 2-15

26th June, Gaelic Grounds:
Tipperary 3-10   Limerick 2-12

26th June, Dr. Cullen Park:
Kilkenny 4-22   Dublin 0-8

26th June, McKenna Park:
Galway 5-19   Down 1-14

ROUND TWO NOT APPLICABLE AS GALWAY WON THEIR OPENING GAME AGAINST DOWN

10th July, Fitzgerald Stadium:
Cork 2-19   Tipperary 1-16

11th July, Semple Stadium:
Kilkenny 4-20   Galway 1-10

17th July, Gaelic Grounds:
Clare 3-16   Offaly 2-10

ALL-IRELAND SENIOR HURLING CHAMPIONSHIP QUALIFIER PRELIMINARY ROUND

LAOIS VERSUS WESTMEATH
O'MOORE PARK (PORTLAOISE)
REFEREE: EAMONN MORRIS (DUBLIN)
RESULT: LAOIS 3-13 WESTMEATH 4-5

SCORERS – LAOIS: Damien Culleton 2-1; Damien Walsh 0-6; David Cuddy 1-1; James Young 0-3; Eoin Browne 0-1; Michael McEvoy 0-1

SCORERS – WESTMEATH: Andrew Mitchell 1-4; Killian Cosgrove 1-0; Ronan Whelan 1-0; Derek McNicholas 1-0; Darren McCormack 0-1

LAOIS
Kevin Galvin

Lar Mahon   Paul Cuddy   Alan Delaney

Joe Fitzpatrick   Liam Tynan   Michael McEvoy

James Young   James Walsh

Eoin Browne   Pat Mahon   Cyril Cuddy

Tommy Fitzgerald   David Cuddy (*Captain*)   Damien Culleton

SUBSTITUTES: Damien Walsh for Pat Mahon; Robert Jones for James Walsh; Rory Conroy for Alan Delaney; Canice Coonan for Eoin Browne; Eamonn Jackman for Tommy Fitzgerald

WESTMEATH
Mark Briody

Dermot Curley   Brendan Murtagh   Paul Greville

Ollie Devine   Christo Murtagh   Darren McCormack (*Captain*)

Shane McDonnell   Enda Loughlin

Killian Cosgrove   Vincent Bateman   Andrew Mitchell

Barry Kennedy   John Shaw   Ronan Whelan

SUBSTITUTES: Derek Gallagher for Paul Greville; Brian Connaughton for Enda Loughlin; Jonathan Forbes for Barry Kennedy; Derek McNicholas for Ronan Whelan

ALL-IRELAND SENIOR HURLING CHAMPIONSHIP QUALIFIER ROUND ONE

CLARE VERSUS LAOIS
GAELIC GROUNDS (LIMERICK)
REFEREE: MICHAEL HAVERTY (GALWAY)
RESULT: CLARE 7-19 LAOIS 2-15

SCORERS – CLARE: Niall Gilligan 2-10; Tony Griffin 4-1; David Forde 0-3; Tony Carmody 1-0; Barry Murphy 0-2; Seánie McMahon 0-1; Frank Lohan 0- 1; Gerry Quinn 0-1

SCORERS – LAOIS: Tommy Fitzgerald 2-2; James Young 0-5; David Cuddy 0-4; Cyril Cuddy 0-1; James Dunne 0-1; Robert Jones 0-1; Pat Mahon 0-1

CLARE
Davy Fitzgerald

Tommy Holland   Brian Lohan   Gerry O'Grady

David Hoey   Seánie McMahon (*Captain*)   Alan Markham

Colin Lynch   Diarmuid McMahon

Jamesie O'Connor   Gerry Quinn   Frank Lohan

Niall Gilligan   Tony Griffin   Daithí O'Connell

SUBSTITUTES: David Forde for Daithí O'Connell; Tony Carmody for Brian Lohan; Colm Forde for Tommy Holland; Barry Murphy for Jamesie O'Connor; Brian O'Connell for Diarmuid McMahon

LAOIS
Kevin Galvin

Cyril Cuddy   Paul Cuddy   Darren Rooney

Joe Fitzpatrick   Liam Tynan   Michael McEvoy

James Young   James Walsh

Eoin Browne   Damien Walsh   Canice Coonan

Tommy Fitzgerald   David Cuddy (*Captain*)   Damien Culleton

SUBSTITUTES: James Dunne for Eoin Browne; Robert Jones for James Walsh; Cathal Brophy for Canice Coonan; Lar Mahon for Darren Rooney; Pat Mahon for Damien Walsh

Jamesie O'Connor, Clare

John Mike Dooley, Kerry and Diarmuid O'Sullivan, Cork

At the launch of the 2004 Guinness All-Ireland Hurling Championship: (L to R) Gary Hanniffy, Offaly; Martin Comerford, Kilkenny; Seánie McMahon, Clare; Ken McGrath, Waterford; TJ Ryan, Limerick; Ben O'Connor, Cork; and Ollie Canning, Galway.

ALL–IRELAND SENIOR HURLING CHAMPIONSHIP QUALIFIER ROUND ONE

TIPPERARY VERSUS LIMERICK
GAELIC GROUNDS (LIMERICK)
REFEREE: AODÁN MAC SUIBHNE (DUBLIN)
RESULT: TIPPERARY 3-10 LIMERICK 2-12

SCORERS – TIPPERARY: Seamus Butler 1-2: John Carroll 1-1; Tommy Dunne 1-1; Eoin Kelly 0-3; Colin Morrissey 0-2; Benny Dunne 0-1

SCORERS – LIMERICK: Niall Moran 0-7; Andrew O'Shaughnessy 2-1; Mark Foley 0-1; James O'Brien 0-1; Donal O'Grady 0-1; Pat Tobin 0-1

TIPPERARY

Brendan Cummins

Martin Maher   Philip Maher   Paul Curran

Eamonn Corcoran   Declan Fanning   Diarmuid Fitzgerald

Tommy Dunne (*Captain*)   Colin Morrissey

Paul Kelly   Eddie Enight   Benny Dunne

Seamus Butler   John Carroll   Eoin Kelly

SUBSTITUTES: Brian O'Meara for Eddie Enright; Lar Corbett for Paul Kelly; Tony Scroope for Brian O'Meara; Mark O'Leary for Seamus Butler

LIMERICK

John Cahill

Mickey Cahill   T.J. Ryan (*Captain*)   Damien Reale

Ollie Moran   Brian Geary   Peter Lawlor

Clem Smith   Mark Foley

Michael McKenna   John Paul Sheahan   Niall Moran

Andrew O'Shaughnessy   Seán O'Connor   Donnacha Sheehan

SUBSTITUTES: James O'Brien for John Paul Sheahan; Donie Ryan for Seán O'Connor; Donal O'Grady for Clem Smith; Paul O'Grady for Michael McKenna; Pat Tobin for Donnacha Sheehan

ALL-IRELAND SENIOR HURLING CHAMPIONSHIP QUALIFIER ROUND ONE

KILKENNY VERSUS DUBLIN
DR. CULLEN PARK (CARLOW)
REFEREE: SEAMUS ROCHE (TIPPERARY)
RESULT: KILKENNY 4-22 DUBLIN 0-8

SCORERS – KILKENNY: Henry Shefflin 2-8; Eddie Brennan 1-3; Jimmy Coogan 1-2; D.J. Carey 0-4; Martin Comerford 0-2; Derek Lyng 0-1; James 'Cha' Fitzpatrick 0-1; John Maher 0-1

SCORERS – DUBLIN: Aodhán de Paor 0-3; David O'Callaghan 0-2; Ronan Fallon 0-1; Seán O'Shea 0-1; Gearóid O'Meara 0-1

KILKENNY
James McGarry
Mark Phelan   Noel Hickey   Tommy Walsh
Richie Mullally   Peter Barry   J.J. Delaney
Derek Lyng   Ken Coogan
Martin Comerford (*Captain*)   Jimmy Coogan   Eddie Brennan
Aidan Fogarty   D.J. Carey   Henry Shefflin

SUBSTITUTES: James 'Cha' Fitzpatrick for Aidan Fogarty; John Maher for D.J. Carey; James Ryall for Peter Barry; Seán Dowling for Derek Lyng; Conor Phelan for Eddie Brennan

DUBLIN
Gary Maguire
Philly Brennan   Stephen Perkins (*Captain*)   Simon Daly
Stephen Hiney   Ronan Fallon   Kevin Ryan
Aodhán de Paor   Carl Meehan
Seán O'Shea   Gearóid Keogh   Seán McCann
David O'Callaghan   Michael Carton   Padraig Fleury

SUBSTITUTES: David Kirwan for Seán McCann; Cormac O'Brien for Philly Brennan; Risteard Brennan for Carl Meehan; Ger O'Meara for Kevin Ryan; Maghnus Breathnach for Gearóid Keogh

ALL-IRELAND SENIOR HURLING CHAMPIONSHIP QUALIFIER ROUND ONE

GALWAY VERSUS DOWN
MCKENNA PARK (BALLYCRAN)
REFEREE: PAT HORAN (OFFALY)
RESULT: GALWAY 5-19 DOWN 1-14

SCORERS – GALWAY: Eugene Cloonan 4-7; Alan Kerins 1-2; David Forde 0-3; David Tierney 0-2; Damien Hayes 0-2; Mark Kerins 0-1; David Hayes 0-1; Kevin Broderick 0-1

SCORERS – DOWN: Stephen Clarke 0-5; Martin Coulter (Junior) 1-2; Andy Savage 0-2; Brendan McGourty 0-2; Gareth Johnson 0-2; Gerard McGrattan 0-1

GALWAY
Liam Donoghue

Damien Joyce   Diarmuid Cloonan   Ollie Canning (*Captain*)

Derek Hardiman   David Collins   Fergal Moore

Fergal Healy   David Hayes

Alan Kerins   David Forde   David Tierney

Damien Hayes   Eugene Cloonan   Kevin Broderick

SUBSTITUTES: Mark Kerins for Kevin Broderick; Tony Óg Regan for David Collins; Rory Gantley for David Hayes; Shane Kavanagh for Derek Hardiman; John Conroy for Fergal Healy

DOWN
Graham Clarke

Michael Braniff   Emmett Dorrian   Andy Bell

Liam Clarke   Gary Savage   Gabriel Clarke

Gerard Adair   Andy Savage

Gerard McGrattan   John Convery   Brendan McGourty

Martin Coulter (Junior) (*Captain*)   Gareth Johnson   Stephen Clarke

SUBSTITUTE: Ryan Conlon for Michael Braniff

Eugene Cloonan, Galway

Ollie Canning, Galway

ALL-IRELAND SENIOR HURLING CHAMPIONSHIP QUALIFIER ROUND THREE

CORK VERSUS TIPPERARY
FITZGERALD STADIUM (KILLARNEY)
REFEREE: BARRY KELLY (WESTMEATH)
RESULT: CORK 2–19 TIPPERARY 1–16

SCORERS – CORK: Joe Deane 0-7; Niall McCarthy 1-2; Ben O'Connor 0-4; Timmy McCarthy 1-1; Kieran Murphy 0-2; Jerry O'Connor 0-1; John Gardiner 0-1; Mickey O'Connell 0-1

SCORERS – TIPPERARY: Eoin Kelly 0-9; Benny Dunne 0-3; Paul Kelly 1-0; Conor Gleeson 0-1; Colin Morrissey 0-1; John Carroll 0-1; Mark O'Leary 0-1

CORK
Donal Óg Cusack

Brian Murphy   Diarmuid O'Sullivan   Wayne Sherlock

John Gardiner   Ronan Curran   Seán Óg Ó hAilpín

Tom Kenny   Jerry O'Connor

Ben O'Connor (*Captain*)   Niall McCarthy   Garvan McCarthy

Kieran Murphy   Brian Corcoran   Joe Deane

SUBSTITUTES: Timmy McCarthy for Garvan McCarthy; Mickey O'Connell for Tom Kenny

TIPPERARY
Brendan Cummins

Martin Maher   Philip Maher   Paul Curran

Eamonn Corcoran   Declan Fanning   Diarmuid Fitzgerald

Colin Morrissey   Tommy Dunne (*Captain*)

Paul Kelly   Conor Gleeson   Benny Dunne

Eoin Kelly   John Carroll   Seamus Butler

SUBSTITUTES: Lar Corbett for Seamus Butler; Mark O'Leary for Paul Kelly; Noel Morris for John Carroll

ALL-IRELAND SENIOR HURLING CHAMPIONSHIP QUALIFIER ROUND THREE

KILKENNY VERSUS GALWAY
SEMPLE STADIUM (THURLES)
REFEREE: DIARMUID KIRWAN (CORK)
RESULT: KILKENNY 4-20 GALWAY 1-10

SCORERS – KILKENNY: Henry Shefflin 2-11; Eddie Brennan 1-3; John Hoyne 1-0; Martin Comerford 0-2; Richie Mullally 0-1; D.J. Carey 0-1; Derek Lyng 0-1; Conor Phelan 0-1

SCORERS – GALWAY: Eugene Cloonan 0-7; Damien Hayes 1-2; Kevin Broderick 0-1

KILKENNY
James McGarry

James Ryall   Noel Hickey   Tommy Walsh

Richie Mullally   Peter Barry   J.J. Delaney

Derek Lyng   Ken Coogan

Martin Comerford (*Captain*)   Henry Shefflin   Conor Phelan

Eddie Brennan   D.J. Carey   Jimmy Coogan

SUBSTITUTE: John Hoyne for Martin Comerford

GALWAY
Liam Donoghue

Damien Joyce   Diarmuid Cloonan   Ollie Canning (*Captain*)

Derek Hardiman   David Hayes   Fergal Moore

Fergal Healy   Tony Óg Regan

Alan Kerins   David Forde   David Tierney

Damien Hayes   Eugene Cloonan   Kevin Broderick

SUBSTITUTES: Adrian Cullinane for Fergal Healy; David Collins for Alan Kerins; Mark Kerins for David Tierney

ALL–IRELAND SENIOR HURLING CHAMPIONSHIP QUALIFIER ROUND THREE

CLARE VERSUS OFFALY
GAELIC GROUNDS (LIMERICK)
REFEREE: PAT O'CONNOR (LIMERICK)
RESULT: CLARE 3-16 OFFALY 2-10

SCORERS – CLARE: Niall Gilligan 2-7; Tony Griffin 1-2; David Forde 0-2; Andrew Quinn 0-2; Tony Carmody 0-1; Colin Lynch 0-1; Daithí O'Connell 0-1

SCORERS – OFFALY: Damien Murray 1-3; Rory Hanniffy 1-2; Brendan Murphy 0-1; Michael Cordial 0-1; Dylan Hayden 0-1; Barry Whelahan 0-1; Gary Hanniffy 0-1

CLARE
Davy Fitzgerald

Brian Quinn   Brian Lohan   Gerry O'Grady

David Hoey   Seánie McMahon (*Captain*)   Alan Markham

Colin Lynch   Diarmuid McMahon

Frank Lohan   Andrew Quinn   David Forde

Niall Gilligan   Tony Griffin   Tony Carmody

SUBSTITUTES: Daithí O'Connell for Brian Lohan; Ollie Baker for Diarmuid McMahon; Jamesie O'Connor for Tony Carmody; Barry Murphy for Tony Griffin; Brian O'Connell for Alan Markham

OFFALY
Brian Mullins

Barry Teehan   Ger Oakley   David Franks

Kevin Brady   Niall Claffey   Colm Cassidy

Michael Cordial   Barry Whelahan

Gary Hanniffy (*Captain*)   Joe Brady   Rory Hanniffy

Brendan Murphy   Neville Coughlan   Damien Murray

SUBSTITUTES: Dylan Hayden for Joe Brady; Stephen Brown for Kevin Brady; Nigel Mannion for Neville Coughlan; Richie McRedmond for Damien Murray

Niall Gilligan, Clare

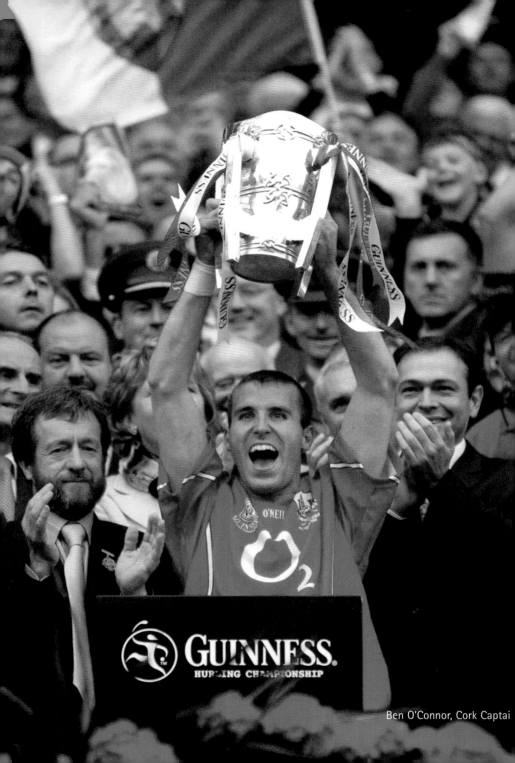

Ben O'Connor, Cork Captai

Sharkey Sports

CASTLE STREET, ARDEE, CO. LOUTH. TEL (041) 685 7300
PROPRIETOR: NIALL SHARKEY

All top brands including

adidas predator • adidas world cup
puma kings • reebok • ellesse • umbro
puma • fila • o'neills • speedo

GAA and Soccer kits at keenest prices guaranteed

Club specials on request

Sharkey Sports

FOR BEST PRICES ON
FOOTBALL BOOTS AND KITS

ALL-IRELAND FINALS SCOREBOARD 2004

March 17th – Croke Park:
All-Ireland Club Football Final: Caltra 0-13 An Ghaeltacht 0-12
All-Ireland Club Hurling Final: Newtownshandrum 0-17 Dunloy 1-6

August 22nd – Croke Park:
Tommy Murphy Cup Final: Clare 1-11 Sligo 0-11

September 12th – Croke Park:
Senior Hurling Final: Cork: 0-17 Kilkenny 0-9
Minor Hurling Final: Galway 3-12 Kilkenny 1-18 (A Draw)

September 18th – Nowlan Park:
Under 21 Hurling Final: Kilkenny 3-21 Tipperary 1-6

September 19th – O'Connor Park:
Minor Hurling Final: Galway 0-16 Kilkenny 1-12 (Replay)

September 19th – Croke Park:
Senior Camogie Final: Tipperary 2-11 Cork 0-9

September 26th – Croke Park:
Senior Football Final: Kerry 1-20 Mayo 2-9
Minor Football Final: Tyrone 0-12 Kerry 0-10

October 2nd - Kingspan Breffni Park:
Under 21 Football Final: Armagh 2-8 Mayo 1-9

October 3rd – Croke Park:
Ladies Senior Football Final: Galway 3-9 Dublin 0-11

13 May 2000: Cormac McAnallen lifts the All-Ireland U21 Cup as Tyrone captain

Remembering Cormac McAnallen

A TRIBUTE BY TYRONE MANAGER, MICKEY HARTE

The morning of March 2nd 2004 will be forever etched in my memory. At 5.30am, Marion and I awoke to the sound of the telephone ringing – an experience that sends a shudder through the heart of every parent whose children are out for the night and have still not returned home. In our specific case, three of our children were at home, so our attention immediately focussed on the one in Belfast. Scarcely before there was time to further process our personal situation, the caller, Paudge Quinn, conveyed the terrible news that Cormac McAnallen was dead. My first instinct was that a road accident had claimed another young vibrant life – an amazing and brilliant young man with so much to give. The shock became even more acute when it emerged that Cormac had in fact died at home in his own bed.

Immediately our thoughts turned to Brendan and Bridget, Cormac's mum and dad and his brothers Donal and Fergus. This was no ordinary son or brother; this was Cormac McAnallen, the young man everyone would have treasured as a member of their family. In the same instant, our hearts also went out to Ashlene, Cormac's fiancée. A few short months previously, we had enjoyed a team holiday in Dubai where we admired their independence as a beautiful young couple and their ability to mix and enjoy group company when that was their preferred option.

Cormac's achievements on the playing field are already well documented and are of such significance that his family can forever be rightly proud. He relished the opportunity to represent Ireland in the International Rules against Australia and his province at Gaelic Football. Cormac also excelled in schools football and at club and college level. He picked up a host of individual awards, including the 'Young Player of the Year' in 2001 and an All-Star in 2003. But, undoubtedly, his greatest accomplishments in a sporting context were in the Tír Eoghain jersey. During the Cormac years, Tír Eoghain participated in ten football competitions at full representative level: the Ulster Minor League, the Ulster Minor Championship; the All-Ireland series and at Under 21 level, the Hastings Cup, the Ulster Championship and the All-Ireland series. In the senior grade, there was the McKenna Cup, the Ulster Championship, the National Football League and the All-Ireland - the Sam Maguire. Not only did Cormac collect a winner's medal in all of those competitions but he also had the unique distinction of captaining Tír Eoghain to no less than seven of those titles. Having just taken over the captaincy of the senior team at the young age of twenty-four, the raising of all ten cups was a distinct possibility.

The achievements of Cormac the man are absolutely breathtaking, but even

Cormac receiving his All Star Award from GAA President, Seán Kelly

more remarkable is how he made them all happen. This is not a reflection on the life of an athlete born with all the natural silky skills associated with greatness. No, this is the story of a young man who was pushing to be in the top five of his local club, Eglish, St. Patrick's at the age of fifteen. This was a young man who forfeited much in 'natural talent' to many of his contemporaries at various stages of his development, yet by the age of twenty-four the package that was Cormac McAnallen reigned supreme. This interpretation in no way diminishes the talents that Cormac possessed in abundance, rather it asks us all to re-appraise what exactly we mean by 'natural talent' and how useful is the current application of that term in the pursuit of excellence.

In life, we all need role models. In the modern era, many acquire the title with dubious credentials – thank God for lives such as Cormac McAnallen's. Always respectful of people, ever determined to challenge and stretch himself, Cormac epitomised Aristotle's definition of excellence, 'we are what we repeatedly do, excellence therefore is not an act but a habit'. Cormac loved all challenges – he was an All-Ireland champion in Scór na nÓg (Tráth na gCeist), and in television's 'Blackboard Jungle', he was a winner on the St. Patrick's, Armagh school team. Cormac

15 February 2004: Cormac leads the Tyrone team onto the field against Longford in the Allianz National Football League

even relished the brain teasers my younger children, Michaela and Matthew used to give him after training or on coach journeys.

All of us, who knew Cormac, hold many memories that enrich our lives. My abiding visions are the focused eyes searching for any potential nugget of self-improvement allied to that angelic smile of satisfaction in times of significant achievement. His attention to detail, his sheer determination, his wonderful use of the talents God gave him and his absolute humility, will no doubt continue to be appreciated on both sides of the heavenly divide.

Arguably, one of the best performances ever given by a Tír Eoghain team was that McKenna Cup victory in late February '04 at Ballybofey. We all celebrated an almost perfect victory. We all hoped it was the beginning of the completion of Cormac's haul of Cups. Sadly all our dreams were soon to be shattered but none more than those of the McAnallen family and Cormac's fiancée, Ashlene. In a footballing context, we had hoped to achieve much at senior level. However, after March 2nd 2004, it seems most appropriate that rather than celebrate collecting pieces of silverware, we should celebrate the special life that was Cormac McAnallen.

Ar dheis Dé go raibh a anam.

Top left: 1998 Cormac lifting the All-Ireland Minor Cup. Top right: 2000, a study in concentration.
Bottom left: 2001, leading the charge.   Bottom right: November 2002, Cormac in his UCD colours.

Photographs: Sportsfile.com

Cormac with his fiancée Ashlene
Photo: Sportsfile.com

Cormac McAnallen and Mickey Harte hold the McKenna Cup – Tyrone's only senior title in 2004
Photograph: Russell Pritchard

Opposite page: GAA President Seán Kelly takes part in the warm-up with Cormac McAnaller during a training session ahead of the International Rules game against Australia in Perth 2003
Photograph: Sportsfile.com

SEÁN KELLY
UACHTARÁN CUMANN LUTHCHLEAS GAEL
in an interview with Brian Carthy

HOMEPLACE: Knockataggle, Kilcummin, Killarney, County Kerry

BORN: April 26, 1952

EDUCATION: Kilcummin National School; Tralee C.B.S.; St. Brendan's College, Killarney; St. Pat's College of Education in Drumcondra, Dublin; U.C.D.

EMPLOYMENT: Taught in Cromcastle Green, Kilmore West, Dublin 5, St. Brendan's College, Killarney

PLAYING CAREER: Played football with Kilcummin; East Kerry; Parnell's of Dublin; Played hurling with St. Pat's, East Kerry

G.A.A. ADMINISTRATION: Chairman of the Kilcummin Club; Chairman of East Kerry Board Na nÓg; Chairman East Kerry Senior Board; Vice Chairman & Chairman of the Kerry County Board; Vice Chairman & Chairman of the Munster Council; President of the G.A.A.

FAMILY: Married to Juliette McNeice from Fair Hill, Killarney. Children – Padraig, Muiread, Laurence and Juliette

WHAT THE G.A.A. PRESIDENT HAS TO SAY

ON HOW HE FIRST BECAME INVOLVED IN THE G.A.A:
Gaelic Football was the only pastime in rural Kerry in the sixties, so I played and followed the game. When I qualified as a teacher and taught in Cromcastle Green in Dublin, I introduced Gaelic Football to the school and naturally started training teams. A Kerry man Jimmy O'Grady and myself trained teams and Parnell's G.A.A. Club took the school on board. We won a County Under 11 title. When I returned to Kerry in 1975, I was asked to become Chairman of East Kerry, Board Na nÓg and I reluctantly accepted the position and my administrative career has continued ever since.

ON THE ROLE OF THE G.A.A. IN IRISH SOCIETY:
Recently, I was invited to go before a Dáil Committee on volunteerism and discuss the G.A.A. Each T.D. and Senator praised the central role of the G.A.A. for providing healthy

pastimes for our youth, enhancing communities, creating a sense of place and providing outstanding facilities in every parish and corner of Ireland. It has been said that over the years, successive governments didn't have a sports policy. They didn't need one as the G.A.A. acting in a totally voluntary capacity provided the policy and the infrastructure. For many, the G.A.A. is still the most powerful influence in Irish society.

ON THE CONTROVERSIAL RULE 42, WHICH PROHIBITS THE USE OF CROKE PARK FOR OTHER SPORTS:

Croke Park is a huge asset, which cost €260 million to refurbish. Apart from a few games, it's closed from October until June. I wouldn't give somebody a twelve-month wage for four months work. Croke Park should be made work to provide revenue for the grassroots. It's totally different to any other ground and could showcase to the world what a great organisation the G.A.A. is and what wonderful progress this country has made. I respect and understand those who disagree with my views because many of my own friends and family members hold similar views. Indeed, I would have felt somewhat the same myself some twenty years ago. But as time goes by, I see a different Ireland, a different world. We are more open and confident now.

ON HIS SUPPORT FOR THE PROPOSAL TO CHANGE THE RULE:

Yes, I am all for change. I said that before I was elected and have reiterated it several times since taking office. When Lansdowne Road is being refurbished, our competitors, but also fellow sportsmen, will have to play their 'home' games abroad. It's not the responsibility of the G.A.A. but neither is the famine in Darfur. Giving a helping hand is part of our human nature.

ON THE VIEW THAT CONGRESS HAS LOST ITS INFLUENCE AS A DECISION MAKING BODY:

If Congress had lost its power, how come Rule 21 was abolished? How were the Hurling Development Committee's proposals brought in? Why was there such a furore when Rule 42 didn't make it to Congress last year? Congress is the only body that can make a change of rule. It's as powerful as ever in that regard.

ON WHETHER THE GAA HAS BEEN GIVEN THE CREDIT FOR THEIR INVESTMENT IN THE MULTI MILLION EURO CROKE PARK STADIUM:

Yes, the G.A.A. has been given credit for its foresight and courage in developing Croke Park. The G.A.A. has the respect of more people in Irish society as a result of the development of Croke Park than ever before. It's 'cool' to visit Croke Park now for matches. People love coming here for conferences as well. Croke Park is a brand name and a buzzword. People see it as the reflection of all that is good in modern Ireland and all achieved by a voluntary organisation in a most cost effective way, while millions upon millions has been wasted and robbed from the public purse in so many ways.

ON THE RECENT €40 MILLION FROM THE GOVERNMENT TOWARDS CROKE PARK:
This was great news for the G.A.A. and great credit is due to the government for honouring an outstanding debt. It was a major bone of contention for many G.A.A. members. The Minister for Sport, John O'Donoghue and the former Minister for Finance, Charlie McCreevy worked very closely with me for a number of months to bring about the desired result. I told them from the outset that there could be no strings attached and they accepted that. I thought the very most that they could pull off was €20 million but thanks to their good work and that of An Taoiseach and Tanáiste, we got the outstanding 38 million plus two for good measure. 2 million, in itself, is a lot of money. It should be remembered as well, even though nobody but nobody commented on it, that in the 'old agreement', the G.A.A. had committed itself to playing several matches in the proposed Abbotstown Stadium – matches that would otherwise be played in Croke Park. That stipulation is also gone, resulting in another huge gain for the G.A.A., as we can play all our games now wherever we like.

ON THE INCREASING LEVELS OF VIOLENCE ON THE FIELD OF PLAY:
Violence is always to be condemned and not just condemned but punished as well. Things tend to go in cycles and there have been far too many unacceptable incidents occurring in recent times. It's hard to know whether it's the increasing profile that the G.A.A. enjoys that causes such incidents to be highlighted. In other words, was it as bad or worse before, but didn't get the same publicity? Either way, violence must be rooted out, as it should have no place in a voluntary sporting body. First of all, clubs must have a code of conduct and insist on standards from all members and players. Disciplinary committees must have the guts to stand by the referee and deal fairly but firmly with everyone, whether they are high or low profile players. I have been working hard at national level since elected to reform our whole disciplinary system. I hope to have radical proposals for next year's Congress in that regard including dividing G.A.C. into separate disciplinary and fixture bodies, introducing a meaningful appeals system and also an independent tribunal.

ON THE CLUB COUNTY DIVIDE AND THE FACT THAT THE HUGE NUMBER OF INTER COUNTY CHAMPIONSHIP GAMES PLAYED HAS SUCH A NEGATIVE IMPACT ON CLUB FIXTURES:
It should be accepted that it is a great honour for a club to have a county player and it is. That honour comes with a price – the player can't be expected to play and train with club and county all the time. Both club and county will get the best out of the player by treating him properly, not forcing him to choose and recognising his particular circumstances. Inter-county games have grown in recent years and will do so again next year. But we have now reached the optimum at inter-county level. It amazes me that successful counties like Kerry and Cork seem to be able to get the balance fairly right and also get their club games played. This year it was disgusting to hear counties who had won nothing for thirty years say that they couldn't compete in

the Tommy Murphy Cup because it would cause major problems for their club fixtures. Good planning and an assumption of success should be the pre-requisites for any county. I set up a task force this year to monitor the amount of club games played and they have now almost completed their task. Their finding will provide us with useful information.

ON WHAT CAN BE DONE TO REMEDY THE PROBLEMS ENCOUNTERED BY PLAYERS ON THE CROKE PARK PITCH. IS IT A SUITABLE SURFACE FOR FOOTBALLERS AND HURLERS?

There are problems with the Croke Park surface, but now like any good story they have been exaggerated out of all proportion. Everybody now is so conscious of it that every slip is a massive problem. The Aussies who came here, unaware of any problems, did not notice any either. So, perception, perception, perception, perhaps, but perhaps not. I can assure you, it is high on our agenda and we are busily monitoring and comparing Croke Park to other grounds. We intend to consult players and managers and examine types of footwear worn. One thing for sure, Croke Park, being the Mecca of Gaelic Games, must have the best possible surface as well, and it will too.

ON THE DWINDLING NUMBER OF PEOPLE GETTING INVOLVED IN CLUB ADMINSTRATION:

Recently, I launched the Club Planning & Administration project in Croke Park. Basically, we intend to visit every club in the country three times between now and 2007 to ensure best practices are carried out. Volunteers will be available to the G.A.A. once things are done properly. Recent political history has shown us that bad men or thugs gather bad men or thugs around them. If our clubs are run properly, with equal opportunity and encouragement to men and women, young and old, then every single one of them can improve. Time is precious but with proper planning, recognition and the right atmosphere in our clubs, people will flock to them.

ON ADVICE TO THOSE CONSIDERING GETTING INVOLVED IN ADMINSTRATION:

You shouldn't be getting involved if you are only concerned with what you will get out of it. Our Lord said: 'In giving you receive'. Every person involved, will tell you that they get far more out of the G.A.A. than they put in – satisfaction of seeing their home club doing well, friendships and a safe happy environment for all concerned. Still, everybody likes a bit of praise and recognition. The A.I.B. Club of the Year and my own President's Awards are aimed at showing appreciation of the volunteer in our organisation, the men and women that have made us what we are, which is the greatest voluntary organisation in the world. Recognition and appreciation are both very important.

ON THE PERCEIVED THREAT TO THE FUTURE OF THE GAA FROM OTHER SPORTS:

It's not as bad as I thought a few years ago. There is room for us all and all sports are good. There is nothing wrong with following cross channel soccer. I have followed Newcastle United, especially Alan Shearer for a long time. Still, it is our own club and our own county that appeals to us most. If our children are properly coached and have a good games schedule, we will hold on to most of them. Competition is the life of trade and it will make us work harder as well. We have the facilities, tradition and support to hold our own and even grow into the future.

ON THE STANDARD OF REFEREEING AND ON THE THREAT TO THE GAME POSED BY THE UNWILLINGNESS OF PEOPLE TO GET INVOLVED IN REFEREEING:

Referees are a special breed – men and women of great courage and commitment. We have made huge strides at National level in promoting and recognising referees. This year alone, I sanctioned boots and new gear for all our inter-county referees and also held a banquet for them. I'd love if we had more respect for referees at all levels. From Under 10 level up, we must encourage that respect from parents and players. Recruitment of referees is vital and it is ongoing. The standard has improved also even though Gaelic Games, because of their speed and physical nature, are always going to be hard to referee. You'll never get a perfect referee, even though we have millions of perfect arm-chair critics.

ON THE FUTURE OF THE INTERNATIONAL RULES:

International Rules is a great concept and a great game. We had 60,000 in Croke Park for the Second Test, which was a foregone conclusion while on the same day the F.A.I. had about 9,000 for their Cup Final. That shows how attractive the International Rules games are to the public – the paying public are no fools. It is also great to be exposed to different cultures and different ways of thinking and doing things. I found the Aussies very interesting and great craic. Irish manager, Pete McGrath and his selectors did a massive job this year and, as I was responsible for appointing them, I was very pleased and proud. Next year is going to be even more challenging in Australia. Did you ever hear about the wounded lion? Australia is the wounded lion now, so roll on October 2005!

ON THE ISSUE OF PROFESSIONALISM WITHIN THE G.A.A. WILL PLAYERS EVENTUALLY BE PAID FOR PLAYING HURLING AND FOOTBALL?

Professionalism is a dead duck as far as the G.A.A. is concerned, despite the best efforts of people who are themselves being paid for what they write and say, telling us otherwise. The day the inter-county player has no affinity to his club or county, the G.A.A. will die. Professionalism is about one God – money - and where that God holds sway, we have great exploitation and corruption all in the name of sport. God help us! Why change something great for something worse?

ON THE ISSUE OF ALLEGED PAYMENTS TO SOME INTER-COUNTY AND CLUB MANAGERS:

Managers have a key role to play in the preparation and performance of any team. They have a lot of work to do outside of formal training times, especially in contacting players, fellow team officials, assessing the opposition and studying videos. Nobody objects to recognising this – but within the amateur code. Most managers and trainers observe this rule at juvenile, school, club and hopefully all levels.

One hears frequent rumours about managers and indeed others also getting 'paid', looking for a 'professional fee' and knowing their 'market value'. This is all what we call in Kerry 'handy talk'. The evidence is not easily unearthed but it's up to club and county officials to ensure that 'reasonable expenses' don't become 'exorbitant expenses' and that 'amateur' doesn't become 'professional'.

At Inter-County level, each manager appointed has to be sanctioned by An Coiste Bainistí on foot of signed declarations by county officials that the appointments are within the amateur code. Would county officials put their name to a lie? One thing for definite, the four most successful managers this year were not paid – namely, Donal O'Grady, Cork hurling manager; Jack O'Connor, Kerry football manager; Pete McGrath, International Rules manager and Brian McEniff, manager of the Ulster team that won the M Donnelly Interprovincial Football Championship.

ON PLAYER WELFARE:

Yes, players must and hopefully are being treated properly now. The players make a lot of sacrifices, reach high standards and are great role models. The provisions of the player welfare package introduced at my first Central Council meeting as Uachtarán must be implemented fully and hopefully are. Endorsements are allowed and encouraged and if players with high profiles can earn a few bob then that is great. No pay for play but ample recognition otherwise is desirable. Club and counties often give pocket money to players when they go on holidays or get on an international team and I know that players appreciate that very much.

ON WHY THERE IS NO OFFICIAL PLAYERS' COMMITTEE:

I gave players an option of electing a committee when I became Uachtarán but many did not want the hassle of being seen to be in conflict with the G.P.A. and preferred not to be involved. I had no problem with that but there is a Players Committee in every county and that is where the action is.

ON THE ROLE OF THE GPA: IS DESSIE FARRELL AND HIS ASSOCIATION LOOKED ON SUSPICIOUSLY BY THE G.A.A.?

I have found Dessie Farrell to be very fair and reasonable. He was one of the best forwards of our generation and it is good that he is trying to represent players' best interests within the amateur code. There are issues over image rights and matters in the marketing area which have caused difficulties, but that shouldn't or doesn't affect our mutual respect. At the end of the day, we are all members of the G.A.A.

ON WHETHER A G.A.A. PRESIDENT CAN INFLUENCE DECISIONS AND MAKE AN IMPACT:

Absolutely. I have found that overall I've got great co-operation for my initiatives. You can also give great support to clubs, schools and other bodies, all of which I have found very fulfilling. I am only in office eighteen months and I've been able to enact great changes over a whole range of areas.

ON WHETHER A THREE-YEAR TERM IS TOO SHORT FOR A G.A.A. PRESIDENT?
Yes and no! The same term applies to members of management, trustees and chairmen and officers of provincial councils. When you know that you have a set term, you can plan in advance and give 100 per cent for the whole period. That's exactly what I'm doing and I intend to keep going at the same rate until the very last minute of my Presidency. Then I'll turn my attention to something else D.V.

ON HIS MOST SIGNIFICANT ACHIEVEMENTS SO FAR AS G.A.A. PRESIDENT:

- Getting the €40 million from Government
- New Hurling Championships; Junior and inter club championships; club planning and administrator initiative and getting the Dublin S.R.C. back on track. (The whole plan for Dublin will be unveiled shortly)
- Progression integration movement between the Ladies and ourselves
- Development of hurling (New initiative shortly)
- Introducing the Tommy Murphy Cup
- Development of links with overseas especially twinning
- Initiation of new disciplinary system
- Improvement of player welfare
- Development of International Rules and Shinty
- The finalisation of Hill 16 and Northern End
- The Development of Hotel adjacent to Croke Park
- New co-ordinated plan for floodlighting and development of grounds
- Development of marketing and sponsorship deals
- Licencing new gear (Gaelic Gear and Azzuri)

"And standing up for what I believe in and being prepared to say it without fear or favour. Giving the weak an equal voice as the strong. I stand up to those who need to be stood up to and try to be fair to all".

Seán with the St. Brendan's College team, which he trained to win the Russell Cup.
Front Row (extreme left) Colm 'Gooch' Cooper; Seán's own son, Padraig, is 3rd from right middle row
Sean's brother, Fr. Larry is on the extreme right of the middle row while their nephew, Darragh is
sitting in the front row, third from left.

Seán with Fr. Jim Kennelly and the St. Brendan's First Year team

Seán, 7th from left, front row, with the Kilcummin team that won the East Kerry Championship, O'Donoghue Cup, in 1973. (The Club's first title in 48 years). Sean's brothers, Dermot, Padraig, (R.I.P.) a De La Salle Brother, Fr. Larry and Fr. Seamus were all members of the winning team, which was trained by Seán's uncle, Fr. Brian Kelly and captained by the legendary Dan Dwyer.

Seán with his great friend and schoolmate, John O'Keeffe

Seán being presented with an achievement award by the A.S.T.I.
Left to right: Charlie Lennon, Juliette, Seán, P.J. Sheehy and Tim Lynch

Left to right: Former G.A.A. President, Sean McCague, Mick O'Connell, the legendary Kerry footballer and his wonderful son, Diarmuid and G.A.A. President, Seán Kelly at the announcement of the Munster Team of the Millennium

Seán presenting medals to Fossa Under 14 County Champions and proudly shaking hands with his own son, Padraig.

Seán with Olympic silver medallist, Sonia O'Sullivan

Celebration time in the Village Inn, Kilcummin with the G.A.A. President and his friends.

Seán and his young family at home with the Sam Maguire Cup in January 1998.
Back Row, Left to Right: Juliette, Muiread, Seán, Padraig. Front Row: Laurence

Seán and Juliette enjoying a night out in the High Chaparral in Castleisland

Seán and his wife Juliette

Andrew Demetriou, Chief Executive of the A.F.L., An Taoiseach Bertie Ahern T.D. and Seán Kelly, President of the G.A.A., stand for An Taoiseach's salute before the Coca Cola International Rules Series 2004 at Croke Park.   Photograph: Sportsfile.com